Coast Guard Cutter Procurement: Background and Issues for Congress

Ronald O'Rourke
Specialist in Naval Affairs

November 18, 2013

Congressional Research Service

7-5700

www.crs.gov

R42567

Summary

The Coast Guard's program of record (POR) calls for procuring 8 National Security Cutters (NSCs), 25 Offshore Patrol Cutters (OPCs), and 58 Fast Response Cutters (FRCs) as replacements for 90 aging Coast Guard cutters and patrol craft. The NSC, OPC, and FRC programs have a combined estimated acquisition cost of about $21.1 billion, and the Coast Guard's proposed FY2014 budget requests a total of $716 million in acquisition funding for the three programs.

NSCs are the Coast Guard's largest and most capable general-purpose cutters. They have an estimated average procurement cost of about $684 million per ship. The first three are now in service, the fourth, fifth, and sixth are under construction, and long lead time materials (LLTM) for the seventh are being procured. The Coast Guard's proposed FY2014 budget requests $616 million in acquisition funding for the seventh NSC; it does not request any funding for long lead time materials (LLTM) for the eighth NSC, which is scheduled to be procured in FY2015.

OPCs are to be smaller, less expensive, and in some respects less capable than NSCs. They have an estimated average procurement cost of about $484 million per ship. The first OPC is to be procured in FY2017. The Coast Guard's proposed FY2014 budget requests $25 million in acquisition funding for the OPC program.

FRCs are considerably smaller and less expensive than OPCs. They have an estimated average procurement cost of about $73 million per boat. A total of 24 have been funded through FY2013, and the first seven had been commissioned into service as of November 16, 2013. The Coast Guard's proposed FY2014 budget requests $75 million in acquisition funding for two FRCs and associated program costs.

Potential oversight issues for Congress regarding the NSC, OPC, and FRC programs include the following:

- the impact on the NSC, OPC, and FRC programs of the March 1, 2013, sequester on FY2013 funding;

- the potential impact on the NSC, OPC, and FRC programs of a possible sequester on FY2014 funding that might occur in late 2013 or early 2014 under the terms of the Budget Control Act of 2011;

- the adequacy of the Coast Guard's planned NSC, OPC, and FRC procurement quantities;

- the lack of a request in the Coast Guard's proposed FY2014 budget for acquisition funding for long lead time materials (LLTM) to support the procurement of an eighth NSC in FY2015;

- the Coast Guard's FY2014 request for acquisition funding for two (rather than six) FRCs;

- delays, cost growth, and testing issues in the FRC program;

- the $25 million in acquisition funding requested for FY2014 for the OPC program, which is one-half of the $50 million that was projected for FY2014 under the Coast Guard's FY2013 budget submission;

- the Coast Guard's acquisition strategy for the OPC;

- the potential for using multiyear procurement (MYP) in acquiring new cutters;

- whether 8 NSCs, 25 OPCs, and 58 FRCs is the best mix of cutters that could be procured for roughly the same total amount of acquisition funding; and

- the adequacy of information available to Congress to support review and oversight of Coast Guard procurement programs, including cutter procurement programs.

Contents

Figures

Tables

Appendixes

Contacts

Introduction

This report provides background information and potential oversight issues for Congress on the Coast Guard's programs for procuring 8 National Security Cutters (NSCs), 25 Offshore Patrol Cutters (OPCs), and 58 Fast Response Cutters (FRCs). These 91 planned cutters are intended as replacements for 90 aging Coast Guard cutters and patrol craft. The Coast Guard began procuring NSCs and FRCs a few years ago, and the first few NSCs and FRCs are now in service. The Coast Guard plans to begin procuring OPCs within the next few years. The NSC, OPC, and FRC programs have a combined estimated acquisition cost of about $21.1 billion, and the Coast Guard's proposed FY2014 budget requests a total of $716 million in acquisition funding for the three programs.

The issue for Congress is whether to approve, reject, or modify the Coast Guard's funding requests and acquisition strategies for the NSC, OPC, and FRC programs. Congress's decisions on these three programs could substantially affect Coast Guard capabilities and funding requirements, and the U.S. shipbuilding industrial base.

The NSC, OPC, and FRC programs have been subjects of congressional oversight for several years, and were previously covered in an earlier CRS report that is now archived.[1] The Coast Guard's plans for modernizing its fleet of polar icebreakers are covered in a separate CRS report.[2]

Background

Older Ships to Be Replaced by NSCs, OPCs, and FRCs

The 91 planned NSCs, OPCs, and FRCs are intended to replace 90 older Coast Guard ships—the service's 12 high-endurance cutters (WHECs), 29 medium-endurance cutters (WMECs), and 49 110-foot patrol craft (WPBs).[3] The Coast Guard's 12 Hamilton (WHEC-715) class high-endurance cutters entered service between 1967 and 1972.[4] The Coast Guard's 29 medium-endurance cutters include 13 Famous (WMEC-901) class ships that entered service between 1983

---

[1] The earlier report was CRS Report RL33753, *Coast Guard Deepwater Acquisition Programs: Background, Oversight Issues, and Options for Congress*, by Ronald O'Rourke. From the late 1990s until 2007, the Coast Guard's efforts to acquire NSCs, OPCs, and FRCs were parts of a larger, integrated Coast Guard acquisition effort aimed at acquiring several new types of cutters and aircraft that was called the Integrated Deepwater System (IDS) program, or Deepwater for short. In 2007, the Coast Guard broke up the Deepwater effort into a series of individual cutter and aircraft acquisition programs, but continued to use the term Deepwater as a shorthand way of referring collectively to these now-separated programs. In its FY2012 budget submission, the Coast Guard stopped using the term Deepwater entirely as a way of referring to these programs. Congress, in acting on the Coast Guard's proposed FY2012 budget, did not object to ending the use of the term Deepwater. Reflecting this development, CRS Report RL33753, *Coast Guard Deepwater Acquisition Programs: Background, Oversight Issues, and Options for Congress* was archived in early 2012, following final congressional action on the FY2012 budget, and remains available to congressional readers as a source of historical reference information on Deepwater acquisition efforts.

[2] CRS Report RL34391, *Coast Guard Polar Icebreaker Modernization: Background and Issues for Congress*, by Ronald O'Rourke.

[3] In the designations WHEC, WMEC, and WPB, W means Coast Guard ship, HEC stands for high-endurance cutter, MEC stands for medium-endurance cutter, and PB stands for patrol boat.

[4] Hamilton-class cutters are 378 feet long and have a full load displacement of about 3,400 tons.

and 1991,[5] 14 Reliance (WMEC-615) class ships that entered service between 1964 and 1969,[6] and two one-of-a-kind cutters that originally entered service with the Navy in 1944 and 1971 and were later transferred to the Coast Guard.[7] The Coast Guard's 49 110-foot Island (WPB-1301) class patrol boats entered service between 1986 and 1992.[8]

Many of these 90 ships are manpower-intensive and increasingly expensive to maintain, and have features that in some cases are not optimal for performing their assigned missions. Some of them have already been removed from Coast Guard service: eight of the Island-class patrol boats were removed from service in 2007 following an unsuccessful effort to modernize and lengthen them to 123 feet; the one-of-a-kind cutter that originally entered service with the Navy in 1944 was decommissioned in 2011; and Hamilton-class cutters are being decommissioned as new NSCs enter service. A July 2012 Government Accountability Office (GAO) report discusses the generally poor physical condition and declining operational capacity of the Coast Guard's older high-endurance cutters, medium-endurance cutters, and 110-foot patrol craft.[9]

Missions of NSCs, OPCs, and FRCs

NSCs, OPCs, and FRCs, like the ships they are intended to replace, are to be multimission ships for routinely performing 7 of the Coast Guard's 11 statutory missions, including

- search and rescue (SAR);
- drug interdiction;
- migrant interdiction;
- ports, waterways, and coastal security (PWCS);
- protection of living marine resources;
- other/general law enforcement; and
- defense readiness operations.[10]

---

[5] Famous class cutters are 270 feet long and have a full load displacement of about 1,800 tons.

[6] Reliance class cutters are 210 feet long and have a full load displacement of about 1,100 tons.

[7] The two one-of-a-kind cutters are the *Acushnet* (WMEC-167), which originally entered service with the Navy in 1944, and the *Alex Haley* (WMEC-39), which originally entered service with the Navy in 1971. The *Acushnet* served in the Navy from until 1946, when it was transferred to the Coast Guard. The ship was about 214 feet long and had a displacement of about 1,700 tons. The *Alex Haley* served in the Navy until 1996. It was transferred to the Coast Guard in 1997, converted into a cutter, and re-entered service with the Coast Guard in 1999. It is 282 feet long and has a full load displacement of about 2,900 tons.

[8] Island-class boats are 110 feet long and have a full load displacement of about 135 to 170 tons.

[9] Government Accountability Office, *Coast Guard[:]Legacy Vessels' Declining Conditions Reinforce Need for More Realistic Operational Targets*, GAO-12-741, July 2012, 71 pp.

[10] The four statutory Coast Guard missions that are not to be routinely performed by NSCs, OPCs, and FRCs are marine safety, aids to navigation, marine environmental protection, and ice operations. These missions are performed primarily by other Coast Guard ships. The Coast Guard states, however, that "while [NSCs, OPCs, and FRCs] will not routinely conduct [the] Aids to Navigation, Marine Safety, or Marine Environmental Protection missions, they may periodically be called upon to support these missions (i.e., validate the position of an Aid to Navigation, transport personnel or serve as a Command and Control platform for a Marine Safety or Marine Environmental Response mission, etc.)." (Source: Coast Guard information paper provided to CRS on June 1, 2012.)

Smaller Coast Guard patrol craft and boats contribute to the performance of some of these seven missions close to shore. NSCs, OPCs, and FRCs perform them both close to shore and in the deepwater environment, which generally refers to waters more than 50 miles from shore.

NSC Program

National Security Cutters (**Figure 1**), also known as Legend (WMSL-750) class cutters,[11] are the Coast Guard's largest and most capable general-purpose cutters.[12] The Coast Guard's program of record (POR)—the service's list, established in 2004, of planned procurement quantities for various new types of ships and aircraft—calls for procuring 8 NSCs as replacements for the service's 12 Hamilton class high-endurance cutters.

Figure 1. National Security Cutter

Source: U.S. Coast Guard photo accessed May 2, 2012, at http://www.flickr.com/photos/coast_guard/5617034780/sizes/l/in/set-72157629650794895/.

Although the NSC program's official total acquisition cost estimate is $4.749 billion, or an average of about $594 million per ship,[13] the Coast Guard more recently estimated the combined

---

[11] In the designation WMSL, W means Coast Guard ship and MSL stands for maritime security cutter, large. NSCs are being named for legendary Coast Guard personnel.

[12] The Coast Guard's three polar icebreakers are much larger than NSCs, but are designed for a more specialized role of operations in polar waters.

[13] *Department of Homeland Security, United States Coast Guard, Fiscal Year 2013 Congressional Justification*, p. CG-AC&I-12 (pdf page 166 of 400).

procurement cost of the eight ships at $5.474 billion, or an average of about $684 million per ship, assuming the seventh and eighth ships were funded in FY2014 and FY2015, respectively.[14]

The first three are now in service, the fourth, fifth, and sixth are under construction, and long lead time materials (LLTM) for the seventh are being procured.

NSCs are larger and technologically more advanced than Hamilton-class cutters.[15] The Coast Guard states that

> Of the Coast Guard's white-hull patrol cutter fleet, the NSC is the largest and most technologically sophisticated in the Coast Guard. Each NSC is capable of operating in the most demanding open ocean environments, including the hazardous fisheries of the North Pacific and the vast approaches of the Southern Pacific where much of the American narcotics traffic occurs. With robust Command, Control, Communication, Computers, Intelligence, Surveillance and Reconnaissance (C4ISR) equipment, stern boat launch and aviation facilities, as well as long-endurance station keeping, the NSCs are afloat operational-level headquarters for complex law enforcement and national security missions involving multiple Coast Guard and partner agency participation.[16]

NSCs are built by Ingalls Shipbuilding of Pascagoula, MS, a shipyard that forms part of Huntington Ingalls Industries (HII).

Table 1 summarizes acquisition funding for the first six NSCs.

Table 1. NSC Acquisition Funding, by Hull

Millions of then-year dollars, rounded to nearest million

Hull	Fiscal years funded	Total acquisition funding (millions)	Production contract award date	Entered service
1	FY02-FY09 and FY15	$701	FY04	August 2008
2	FY04-FY09 and FY15	$528	FY05	May 2010
3	FY04-FY09	$551	FY07	March 2012
4	FY04-FY10, FY13, FY15-FY16	$690	FY11 (1st Quarter)	
5	FY10-FY11	$697	FY11 (4th Quarter)	
6	FY12 and FY13	$735a		

Source: Coast Guard e-mail to CRS, December 9, 2011, and FY2013 Coast Guard budget submission.

a. Includes $77 million in FY2012 and $658 million requested for FY2013. The FY2013 funding request for the NSC program also includes $25 million for post-production activities for the fourth NSC to replace $25 million in funding for post-production activities provided in FY2010.

The Coast Guard's proposed FY2014 budget requests $616 million in acquisition funding for the seventh NSC; it does not request any funding for long lead time materials (LLTM) for the eighth NSC, which is scheduled to be procured in FY2015.

---

[14] Source: Coast Guard information paper on NSC procurement costs provided to CRS on May 14, 2012.

[15] The NSC design is 418 feet long and has a full load displacement of about 4,500 tons. The displacement of the NSC design is about equal to that of Navy's Oliver Hazard Perry (FFG-7) class frigates, which are 453 feet long and have a full load displacement of about 4,200 tons.

[16] U.S. Coast Guard description of the NSC, accessed April 26, 2013, at http://www.uscg.mil/acquisition/nsc/features.asp.

OPC Program

Offshore Patrol Cutters (**Figure 2**) are to be smaller, less expensive, and in some respects less capable than NSCs. The Coast Guard's POR calls for procuring 25 OPCs as replacements for the service's 29 medium-endurance cutters. Under the Coast Guard's FY2013 five-year (FY2013-FY2017) capital investment plan, the first OPC was to be procured in FY2017.

Figure 2. Offshore Patrol Cutter (Generic Conceptual Rendering)

Source: U.S. Coast Guard generic conceptual rendering accessed May 3, 2012, at http://www.uscg.mil/hq/cg9/opc/default.asp.

The Coast Guard estimates the OPC program's total acquisition cost at $12.101 billion, or an average of about $484 million per ship. These figures reflect a revised OPC program baseline that was approved in April 2012; they represent a 49% increase over the previous figures of $8.098 billion and $324 million, respectively.[17] A September 2012 GAO report states that

> The initial Deepwater baseline included an $8 billion estimate for the Offshore Patrol Cutter program. However, program officials stated they did not have good data for how the lead systems integrator for the Deepwater program generated the original estimate, and that the current estimate approved by DHS in April 2012—with a threshold of approximately $12 billion—is higher likely because the original estimate was developed before the program requirements were established. Program officials also cited delays in the program, and the corresponding inflation associated with those delays, as additional reasons for the cost increase. Even though the Coast Guard used the original 2007 Deepwater Baseline estimate of $8 billion to characterize the expected cost of the program multiple times to Congress, it

---

[17] Government Accountability Office, *Coast Guard[:] Portfolio Management Approach Needed to Improve Major Acquisition Outcomes*, GAO-12-918, September 2012, p. 13 (Figure 13).

now characterizes the revised acquisition program baseline as the initial cost estimate for the program.[18]

The Coast Guard's Request for Proposal (RFP) for the program, released on September 25, 2012, establishes an affordability requirement for the program of an average unit price of $310 million per ship, or less, in then-year dollars (i.e., dollars that are not adjusted for inflation) for ships 4 through 9 in the program.[19] This figure represents the shipbuilder's portion of the total cost of the ship; it does not include the cost of government-furnished equipment (GFE) on the ship,[20] or other program costs—such as those for program management, system integration, and logistics— that contribute to the above-cited figure of $484 million per ship.[21]

The service states that OPCs

> will complement the Coast Guard's current and future fleet to extend the service's operational capabilities. The OPC will replace the service's 210-foot and 270-foot Medium Endurance Cutters. It will feature increased range and endurance, powerful weapons, a larger flight deck, and improved command, control, communications, computers, intelligence, surveillance and reconnaissance (C4ISR) equipment. The OPC will accommodate aircraft and small boat operations in all weather.[22]

At least eight shipyards expressed interest in the program.[23] The Coast Guard's acquisition strategy for the first 9 to 11 ships in the program is as follows:

> The OPC procurement shall implement a two-phase down select strategy. Phase I entails a full and open competition for Preliminary and Contract Design (P&CD) awarded to a maximum of three offerors. The Coast Guard intends to competitively award the Phase I contract in Fiscal Year (FY) 2013. P&CD will culminate in a Contract Design Review (KDR). After KDR, the three contractors will submit proposals which will result in a down selection to one contractor to continue with Phase II.

---

[18] Government Accountability Office, *Coast Guard[:] Portfolio Management Approach Needed to Improve Major Acquisition Outcomes*, GAO-12-918, September 2012, p. 15.

[19] Source: Section C.5 of the RFP, accessed October 31, 2012, at http://www.uscg mil/ACQUISITION/newsroom/ updates/opc092512.asp.

[20] GFE is equipment that the government procures and then delivers to the shipyard for installation on the ship.

[21] Source: Coast Guard emails to CRS dated June 25, 2013.

[22] Coast Guard fact sheet on the OPC accessed April 26, 2013, at http://www.uscg mil/acquisition/opc/pdf/opc.pdf.

[23] The firms are General Dynamics Bath Iron Works (GD/BIW) of Bath, ME; Bollinger Shipyards of St. Rose, LA; Eastern Shipbuilding Group of Panama City, FL; Huntington Ingalls Industries (HII) of Pascagoula, MS; Marinette Marine Corporation of Marinette, WS; General Dynamics National Steel and Shipbuilding Company (GD/NASSCO) of San Diego, CA; Vigor Shipyards of Seattle, WA; and VT Halter Marine of Pascagoula, MS. Source: U. S. Coast Guard Offshore Patrol Cutter (OPC) List of Interested Contractors Updated July 2012, accessed online October 23, 2012, at http://www.uscg.mil/ACQUISITION/opc/pdf/companiesinterested.pdf; and Kevin Brancato and Anne Laurent, *Coast Guard's $12 Billion Cutter Competition Spurs Eight Shipyards to Dive In*, Bloomberg Government Study, November 8, 2012, 6 pp. The Coast Guard document states that these firms "expressed interest in the Offshore Patrol Cutter acquisition and have agreed to their names provided on the Coast Guard website." The Bloomberg Government Study states that "Marinette Marine, owned by Italian shipbuilder Fincantieri, may build its bid based on its version of the Littoral Combat Ship for the U.S. Navy. Vigor Industrial will propose a derivative of a commercial curved-hull design by Norwegian ship maker Ulstein. VT Halter will use Paris-based DCNS as design partner." See also Stew Magnuson, "New Coast Guard Cutter Sparks Fierce Competition Among Shipbuilders," *National Defense* (www.nationaldefensemagazine.org), April 2013, accessed March 26, 2013, at http://www.nationaldefensemagazine.org/archive/2013/April/Pages/ NewCoastGuardCutterSparksFierceCompetitionAmongShipbuilders.aspx.

(h) Phase II award is planned for FY.... Phase II's down selection will be accomplished by exercising one option with a single contractor for Detail Design (DD) with additional options for Long Lead Time Materials, lead ship and eight to ten follow ships. DD will start after option exercise and be complete upon delivery of the first ship. The contractor will present the OPC design at the Initial Critical Design Reviews (ICDR) and Final Critical Design Review (FCDR) followed by a Production Readiness Review (PRR). During Phase II contract performance, the contractor will be encouraged to submit a fixed price proposal (before construction begins on the Hull #6) for option Hulls #6 through #11 (LRIP 2). If the priced effort is deemed fair and reasonable the contractor shall be eligible for Hulls #10 and #11. If not, the contract will continue with the FPI structure and the contract will end with Hull #9.[24]

A September 9, 2013, update from the Coast Guard states:

Following a thorough evaluation of proposals received in response to the Coast Guard's solicitation for preliminary and contract design of the Offshore Patrol Cutter, the Coast Guard determined it is in the government's best interest to hold discussions. In accordance with the Federal Acquisition Regulation, the decision to conduct discussions was accompanied by the establishment of a competitive range comprising the most highly-rated proposals as determined by the evaluation criteria. The Coast Guard will conduct discussions with offerors in the competitive range and provide each a limited opportunity to revise and improve their proposals.

The OPC acquisition is a two-phased competition with a plan to award up to three contracts to competing firms for preliminary and contract design (Phase I) and then down-select to a single contractor for detail design and ship construction (Phase II).

The Coast Guard received proposals on Jan. 23, 2013, and began technical, management, past performance, and price evaluations for Phase I. Evaluation of revised proposals is expected to support an award of contracts for OPC preliminary and contract design in the 2nd quarter of fiscal year 2014.[25]

A September 6, 2013, blog entry states:

The unofficial word is that the Coast Guard has set the competitive range for the OPC program and has thereby eliminated at least three of the competitors—Marinette Marine, NASSCO and Vigor Industrial. If this is the case, that leaves five yards still under consideration for up to three Phase I contracts—two from the "Big Six" [shipyards]—Bath Iron Works and Ingalls Shipbuilding—and three from the "Second Tier" [shipyards]— Bollinger Shipyards, Eastern Shipbuilding and VT Halter Marine.[26]

---

[24] Source: Section C.1 of the RFP, accessed March 26, 2013, at http://www.uscg.mil/ACQUISITION/newsroom/updates/opc092512.asp.

[25] "Acquisition Update: Coast Guard to Hold Discussions with Offerors on OPC Acquisition," September 9, 2013, accessed November 18, 2013, at http://www.uscg mil/acquisition/newsroom/updates/opc090913.asp.

[26] "Coast Guard Cuts OPC Field," September 6, 2013, accessed November 11, 2013, at http://www.coltoncompany.com/newsandcomment/news/2013/09 htm. See also Calvin Biesecker, "Coast Guard Narrows Candidates For Next Cutter, Delays Design Award," *Defense Daily*, September 11, 2013: 3-4; Dennis Hoey, "Bath Iron Works Finalist To Build New Coast Guard Cutters," *Portland (ME) Press Herald* (http://www.pressherald.com/), September 10, 2013; "Bath Iron Works In Running To Build New Coast Guard Vessels," *Bangor Daily News (http:bangordailynews.com)*, September 10, 2013.

The Coast Guard's proposed FY2014 budget requests $25 million in acquisition funding for the OPC program, to be used for technical and project management.

FRC Program

Fast Response Cutters (**Figure 3**), also called Sentinel (WPC-1101) class patrol boats, are considerably smaller and less expensive than OPCs, but are larger than the Coast Guard's older patrol boats.[27] The Coast Guard's POR calls for procuring 58 FRCs as replacements for the service's 49 Island-class patrol boats.

Figure 3. Fast Response Cutter

(With an older Island-class patrol boat behind)

Source: U.S. Coast Guard photo accessed May 4, 2012, at http://www.flickr.com/photos/coast_guard/6871815460/sizes/l/in/set-72157629286167596/.

The Coast Guard states that

> The planned fleet of FRCs will conduct primarily the same missions as the 110' patrol boats being replaced. In addition, the FRC will have several increased capabilities enhancing overall mission execution. The FRC is designed for rapid response, with approximately a 28 knot speed capability, and will typically operate in the coastal zones. Examples of missions that FRCs will complete include SAR, Migrant Interdiction, Drug Interdiction and Ports Waterways and Coastal Security.

---

[27] FRCs are 154 feet long and have a full load displacement of 353 tons.

FRCs will provide enhanced capabilities over the 110's including improved C4ISR capability and interoperability; stern launch and recovery (up through sea state 4) of a 40 knot, Over-the-Horizon, 7m cutter boat; a remote operated, gyro stabilized MK38 Mod 2, 25mm main gun; improved sea keeping; and enhanced crew habitability.[28]

The Coast Guard estimates the FRC program's total acquisition cost at $4.243 billion, or an average of about $73 million per boat.[29] A total of 24 have been funded through FY2013, and the first seven had been commissioned into service as of November 16, 2013. On September 18, 2013, the FRC program received approval from DHS to enter full-rate production.[30] On September 25, 2013, the Coast Guard exercised an option for six FRCs (numbers 19-24 in the program).[31]

FRCs are currently built by Bollinger Shipyards of Lockport, LA. Bollinger's contract with the Coast Guard originally included options to build up to 34 FRCs, but some of the options were not fully exercised by the Coast Guard, so Bollinger's contract can now cover up to 30 FRCs. The builder of the remaining 28 planned FRCs has not yet been determined. The Coast Guard holds the data rights for the Sentinel-class design and plans to hold a competition in 2015 for the contract to build the remaining boats in the class.[32]

Table 2 summarizes acquisition funding for the first 18 FRCs.

Table 2. FRC Acquisition Funding, by Hull

Millions of then-year dollars, rounded to nearest million

Quantity	Hulls	Fiscal years funded	Total acquisition funding (millions)	Average unit cost (millions)
0	n/a	FY07 and prior years	$2	n/a
4	1 to 4	FY05, FY07, FY09	$267	$66.75
4	5 to 8	FY2010	$243	$60.75
4	9 to 12	FY2011	$240	$60.00
4[a]	13 to 16[a]	FY2012	$358[b]	$59.00[b]

Source: Coast Guard e-mail to CRS, December 9, 2011, and FY2013 Coast Guard budget submission.

a. The FY2012 budget funded the procurement of six boats (numbers 13 through 18). The Coast Guard's FY2013 budget proposed deferring the procurement of boats 17 and 18 to FY2013, which would reduce the FY2012 figure to 4 boats (hulls 13 to 16). Under this proposal, of the $358 million provided for the program in FY2012, $95 million provided for boats 17 and 18 would be, in effect, transferred to FY2013.

---

[28] *Department of Homeland Security, United States Coast Guard, Fiscal Year 2013 Congressional Justification*, p. CG-AC&I-28 (pdf page 182 of 400).

[29] Government Accountability Office, *Coast Guard[:] Portfolio Management Approach Needed to Improve Major Acquisition Outcomes*, GAO-12-918, September 2012, p. 13 (Figure 13).

[30] "Acquisition Update: Sentinel-class Fast Response Cutter Project Achieves Acquisition Milestone," September 18, 2013, accessed November 18, 2013, at http://www.uscg.mil/acquisition/newsroom/updates/frc092413.asp.

[31] "Acquisition Update: Contract Option Exercised for Six More Fast Response Cutters," September 25, 2013, accessed November 18, 2013, at http://www.uscg mil/acquisition/newsroom/updates/frc092513.asp.

[32] Mike McCarthy, "House Markup Would Avoid Slipping USCG's New Cutters," *Defense Daily*, May 15, 2012: 3.

b. Includes $27 million for FRC reprocurement data and licensing package (RDLP) and $95 million to be used for procuring two additional FRCs (numbers 17 and 18) in FY2013. These two sums are excluded from the unit cost calculation.

The Coast Guard's proposed FY2014 budget requests $75 million in acquisition funding for two FRCs, associated contact line items, and project management costs.

NSC, OPC, and FRC Funding in FY2013 Five-Year Capital Investment Plan

Table 3 shows annual acquisition funding for the NSC, OPC, and FRC programs in the Coast Guard's FY2013 and FY2014 Five Year Capital Investment Plans (CIPs).

Table 3. NSC, OPC, and FRC Funding in FY2013 and FY2014 Five-Year Capital Investment Plans (CIPs)

(millions of then-year dollars)

	FY2013	FY2014	FY2015	FY2016	FY2017	FY2018
NSC program						
FY13 CIP	683[a]	0	0	0	0	
FY14 CIP		616	710	38	0	45
Difference (common years)		*+616*	*+710*	*+38*	*0*	
OPC program						
FY13 CIP	30	50	40	200[b]	530[c]	
FY14 CIP		25	65	200	530	430
Difference (common years)		*-25*	*+25*	*0*	*0*	
FRC program						
FY13 CIP	139[d]	360	360	360	360	
FY14 CIP		75	110	110	110	110
Difference (common years)		*-285*	*-250*	*-250*	*-250*	
Total						
FY13 CIP	852	410	400	560	890	
FY14 CIP		716	885	348	640	585
Difference (common years)		*+306*	*+485*	*-212*	*-250*	

Source: FY2013 CIP, as shown in *Department of Homeland Security, United States Coast Guard, Fiscal Year 2013 Congressional Justification*, p. CG-AC&I-12 (pdf page 166 of 400); and FY2014 CIP, accessed May 13, 2013, at http://www.uscg.mil/posturestatement/docs/USCG_Capital%20Investment%20Plan_FY14-18.pdf.

a. Includes $658 million to complete acquisition funding for the sixth NSC, and $25 million in post-production activities for the fourth NSC.

b. Includes funding for detailed design and long-lead time materials for the first OPC.

c. Includes funding to complete the acquisition cost of the first OPC.

d. The Coast Guard's FY2013 budget proposes to shift an additional $95 million in FY2012 funding to FY2013, resulting in a total of $234 million available to the FRC program in FY2013.

Issues for Congress

Impact of March 1, 2013, Sequester on FY2013 Funding

One issue for Congress concerns the impact on NSC, OPC, and FRC programs of the March 1, 2013, sequester on FY2013 funding, particularly in terms of the Coast Guard's ability to execute construction work on the sixth NSC and the FRCs that were funded in FY2013.

Potential Impact of Possible Late 2013/Early 2014 Sequester on FY2014 Funding

Another potential issue for Congress concerns the potential impact on the NSC, OPC, and FRC programs of a possible sequester on FY2014 funding that might occur in late 2013 or early 2014 under the terms of the Budget Control Act of 2011 (S. 365/P.L. 112-25 of August 2, 2011).

Adequacy of Planned NSC, OPC, and FRC Procurement Quantities

Another oversight issue for Congress concerns the adequacy of the Coast Guard's planned NSC, OPC, and FRC procurement quantities. The POR's planned force of 91 NSCs, OPCs, and FRCs is about equal in number to the Coast Guard's legacy force of 90 high-endurance cutters, medium-endurance cutters, and 110-foot patrol craft. NSCs, OPCs, and FRCs, moreover, are to be individually more capable than the older ships they are to replace. Even so, Coast Guard studies have concluded that the planned total of 91 NSCs, OPCs, and FRCs would be considerably fewer ships than the number that would be needed to fully perform the service's statutory missions in coming years, in part because Coast Guard mission demands are expected to be greater in coming years than they were in the past. CRS first testified about this issue in 2005.[33]

The Coast Guard estimates that with the POR's planned force of 91 NSCs, OPCs, and FRCs, the service would have capability or capacity gaps[34] in 6 of its 11 statutory missions—search and rescue (SAR); defense readiness; counter-drug operations; ports, waterways, and coastal security (PWCS); protection of living marine resources (LMR); and alien migrant interdiction operations (AMIO). The Coast Guard judges that some of these gaps would be "high risk" or "very high risk."

Public discussions of the POR frequently mention the substantial improvement that the POR force would represent over the legacy force. Only rarely, however, have these discussions explicitly acknowledged the extent to which the POR force would nevertheless be smaller in number than the force that would be required, by Coast Guard estimate, to fully perform the Coast Guard's statutory missions in coming years. Discussions that focus on the POR's improvement over the legacy force while omitting mention of the considerably larger number of

---

[33] See Statement of Ronald O'Rourke, Specialist in National Defense, Congressional Research Service, Before the Senate Commerce, Science, and Transportation Committee, Subcommittee on Fisheries and the Coast Guard, Hearing on The Coast Guard's Revised Deepwater Implementation Plan, June 21, 2005, pp. 1-5.

[34] The Coast Guard uses *capability* as a qualitative term, to refer to the kinds of missions that can be performed, and *capacity* as a quantitative term, to refer to how much (i.e., to what scale or volume) a mission can be performed.

cutters that would be required, by Coast Guard estimate, to fully perform the Coast Guard's statutory missions in coming years could encourage audiences to conclude, contrary to Coast Guard estimates, that the POR's planned force of 91 cutters would be capable of fully performing the Coast Guard's statutory missions in coming years.

In a study completed in December 2009 called the Fleet Mix Analysis (FMA) Phase 1, the Coast Guard calculated the size of the force that in its view would be needed to fully perform the service's statutory missions in coming years. The study refers to this larger force as the objective fleet mix. **Table 4** compares planned numbers of NSCs, OPCs, and FRCs in the POR to those in the objective fleet mix.

Table 4. Program of Record Compared to Objective Fleet Mix

From Fleet Mix Analysis Phase 1 (2009)

Ship type	Program of Record (POR)	Objective Fleet Mix From FMA Phase I	Objective Fleet Mix compared to POR	
			Number	%
NSC	8	9	+1	+13%
OPC	25	57	+32	+128%
FRC	58	91	+33	+57%
Total	**91**	**157**	**+66**	**+73%**

Source: Fleet Mix Analysis Phase I, Executive Summary, Table ES-8 on page ES-13.

As can be seen in **Table 4**, the objective fleet mix includes 66 additional cutters, or about 73% more cutters than in the POR. Stated the other way around, the POR includes about 58% as many cutters as the objective fleet mix.

As intermediate steps between the POR force and the objective fleet mix, FMA Phase 1 calculated three additional forces, called FMA-1, FMA-2, and FMA-3. (The objective fleet mix was then relabeled FMA-4.) **Table 5** compares the POR to FMAs 1 through 4.

Table 5. POR Compared to FMAs I Through 4

From Fleet Mix Analysis Phase 1 (2009)

Ship type	Program of Record (POR)	FMA-I	FMA-2	FMA-3	FMA-4 (Objective Fleet Mix)
NSC	8	9	9	9	9
OPC	25	32	43	50	57
FRC	58	63	75	80	91
Total	**91**	**104**	**127**	**139**	**157**

Source: Fleet Mix Analysis Phase I, Executive Summary, Table ES-8 on page ES-13.

FMA-1 was calculated to address the mission gaps that the Coast Guard judged to be "very high risk." FMA-2 was calculated to address both those gaps and additional gaps that the Coast Guard judged to be "high risk." FMA-3 was calculated to address all those gaps, plus gaps that the Coast

Guard judged to be "medium risk." FMA-4—the objective fleet mix—was calculated to address all the foregoing gaps, plus the remaining gaps, which the Coast Guard judge to be "low risk" or "very low risk." **Table 6** shows the POR and FMAs 1 through 4 in terms of their mission performance gaps.

Table 6. Force Mixes and Mission Performance Gaps

From Fleet Mix Analysis Phase 1 (2009)—an X mark indicates a mission performance gap

Missions with performance gaps	Risk levels of these performance gaps	Program of Record (POR)	FMA-1	FMA-2	FMA-3	FMA-4 (Objective Fleet Mix)
Search and Rescue (SAR) capability	Very high	X				
Defense Readiness capacity	Very high	X				
Counter Drug capacity	Very high	X				
Ports, Waterways, and Coastal Security (PWCS) capacity[a]	High	X	X			
Living Marine Resources (LMR) capability and capacity[a]	High	X	X			[all gaps addressed]
PWCS capacity[b]	Medium	X	X	X		
LMR capacity[c]	Medium	X	X	X		
Alien Migrant Interdiction Operations (AMIO) capacity[d]	Low/very low	X	X	X	X	
PWCS capacity[e]	Low/very low	X	X	X	X	

Source: Fleet Mix Analysis Phase 1, Executive Summary, page ES-11 through ES-13.

Notes: In the first column, The Coast Guard uses *capability* as a qualitative term, to refer to the kinds of missions that can be performed, and *capacity* as a quantitative term, to refer to how much (i.e., to what scale or volume) a mission can be performed.

a.   This gap occurs in the Southeast operating area (Coast Guard Districts 7 and 8) and the Western operating area (Districts 11, 13, and 14).

b.   This gap occurs in Alaska.

c.   This gap occurs in Alaska and in the Northeast operating area (Districts 1 and 5).

d.   This gap occurs in the Southeast and Western operating areas.

e.   This gap occurs in the Northeast operating area.

Figure 4, taken from FMA Phase 1, depicts the overall mission capability/performance gap situation in graphic form. It appears to be conceptual rather than drawn to precise scale. The black line descending toward 0 by the year 2027 shows the declining capability and performance of the Coast Guard's legacy assets as they gradually age out of the force. The purple line branching up from the black line shows the added capability from ships and aircraft to be procured under the POR, including the 91 planned NSCs, OPCs, and FRCs. The level of capability to be provided when the POR force is fully in place is the green line, labeled "2005 Mission Needs Statement." As can be seen in the graph, this level of capability is substantially below a projection of Coast Guard mission demands made after the terrorist attacks of September 11, 2001 (the red line, labeled "Post-9/11 CG Mission Demands"), and even further below a Coast Guard projection of future mission demands (the top dashed line, labeled "Future Mission Demands"). The dashed blue lines show future capability levels that would result from reducing planned procurement quantities in the POR or executing the POR over a longer time period than originally planned.

Figure 4. Projected Mission Demands vs. Projected Capability/Performance

From Fleet Mix Analysis Phase 1, Executive Summary

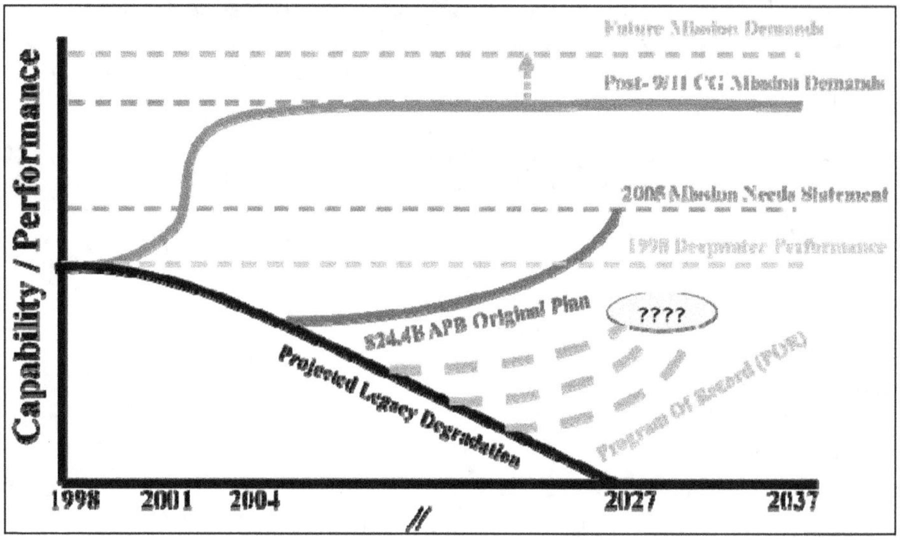

Source: Fleet Mix Analysis Phase 1, Executive Summary, Figure ES-1 on p. ES-2.

FMA Phase 1 was a fiscally unconstrained study, meaning that the larger force mixes shown in **Table 5** were calculated primarily on the basis of their capability for performing missions, rather than their potential acquisition or life-cycle operation and support (O&S) costs.

Although the FMA Phase 1 was completed in December 2009, the figures shown in **Table 5** were generally not included in public discussions of the Coast Guard's future force structure needs until April 2011, when GAO presented them in testimony.[35] GAO again presented them in a July 2011 report.[36]

The Coast Guard completed a follow-on study, called Fleet Mix Analysis (FMA) Phase 2, in May 2011. Among other things, FMA Phase 2 includes a revised and updated objective fleet mix called the refined objective mix. **Table 7** compares the POR to the objective fleet mix from FMA Phase 1 and the refined objective mix from FMA Phase 2.

---

[35] Government Accountability Office, *Coast Guard[:]Observations on Acquisition Management and Efforts to Reassess the Deepwater Program, Testimony Before the Subcommittee on Coast Guard and Maritime Transportation, Committee on Transportation and Infrastructure, House of Representatives, Statement of John P. Hutton, Director Acquisition and Sourcing Management*, GAO-11-535T, April 13, 2011, p. 10.

[36] Government Accountability Office, *Coast Guard[:]Action Needed As Approved Deepwater Program Remains Unachievable*, GAO-11-743, July 2011, p. 46.

Table 7. POR Compared to Objective Mixes in FMA Phases 1 and 2

From Fleet Mix Analysis Phase 1 (2009) and Phase 2 (2011)

Ship type	Program of Record (POR)	Objective Fleet Mix from FMA Phase 1	Refined Objective Mix from FMA Phase 2
NSC	8	9	9
OPC	25	57	49
FRC	58	91	91
Total	**91**	**157**	**149**

Source: Fleet Mix Analysis Phase 1, Executive Summary, Table ES-8 on page ES-13, and Fleet Mix Analysis Phase 2, Table ES-2 on p. iv.

As can be seen in **Table 7**, compared to the objective fleet mix from FMA Phase 1, the refined objective mix from FMA Phase 2 includes 49 OPCs rather than 57. The refined objective mix includes 58 additional cutters, or about 64% more cutters than in the POR. Stated the other way around, the POR includes about 61% as many cutters as the refined objective mix.

Compared to the POR, the larger force mixes shown in **Table 5** and **Table 7** would be more expensive to procure, operate, and support than the POR force. Using the average NSC, OPC, and FRC procurement cost figures presented earlier (see "Background"), procuring the 58 additional cutters in the Refined Objective Mix from FMA Phase 2 might cost an additional $10.7 billion, of which most (about $7.8 billion) would be for the 24 additional FRCs. (The actual cost would depend on numerous factors, such as annual procurement rates.) O&S costs for these 58 additional cutters over their life cycles (including crew costs and periodic ship maintenance costs) would require billions of additional dollars.[37]

The larger force mixes in the FMA Phase 1 and 2 studies, moreover, include not only increased numbers of cutters, but also increased numbers of Coast Guard aircraft. In the FMA Phase 1 study, for example, the objective fleet mix included 479 aircraft—93% more than the 248 aircraft in the POR mix. A decision to procure larger numbers of cutters like those shown in **Table 5** and **Table 7** might thus also imply a decision to procure, operate, and support larger numbers of Coast Guard aircraft, which would require billions of additional dollars. The FMA Phase 1 study estimated the procurement cost of the objective fleet mix of 157 cutters and 479 aircraft at $61 billion to $67 billion in constant FY2009 dollars, or about 66% more than the procurement cost of $37 billion to $40 billion in constant FY2009 dollars estimated for the POR mix of 91 cutters and 248 aircraft. The study estimated the total ownership cost (i.e., procurement plus life-cycle O&S cost) of the objective fleet mix of cutters and aircraft at $201 billion to $208 billion in constant FY2009 dollars, or about 53% more than the total ownership cost of $132 billion to $136 billion in constant FY2009 dollars estimated for POR mix of cutters and aircraft.[38]

---

[37] The FMA Phase 1 and Phase 2 studies present acquisition and life-cycle ownership cost calculations for force mixes that include not only larger numbers of NSC, OPCs, and FRCs, but corresponding larger numbers of Coast Guard aircraft.

[38] Fleet Mix Analysis Phase 1, Executive Summary, Table ES-11 on page ES-19, and Table ES-10 on page ES-18. The life-cycle O&S cost was calculated through 2050.

The POR was originally defined in 2004 as the optimal mix of assets that could be acquired for a total estimated acquisition cost of about $24 billion, and the $24 billion figure is often referenced as a baseline in discussing Coast Guard plans for acquiring new deepwater-capable ships and aircraft. GAO's July 2011 report, for example, notes that the total estimated acquisition cost of the POR has grown to as much as $29.3 billion, or about $5 billion more than the original estimate of $24.2 billion, and that there could be additional cost growth beyond that figure.[39]

GAO has expressed strong doubts, given growth in the estimated acquisition cost of the POR and the amounts of acquisition funding that the Coast Guard has received in recent years, about the Coast Guard's ability to afford the POR, let alone any larger force mix, and has recommended in its July 2011 report and subsequent work that the Coast Guard instead examine force mixes that are smaller than the POR.[40] Force mixes that are smaller than the POR might lead to overall capability levels similar to those shown by the dashed blue lines in **Figure 4**, and mission performance gaps that are greater in magnitude than those indicated for the POR force in **Table 6**.

At a March 7, 2012, hearing before the Oceans, Atmosphere, Fisheries, and Coast Guard subcommittees of the Senate Commerce, Science, and Transportation Committee, Admiral Robert J. Papp, the Commandant of the Coast Guard, in commenting on GAO's July 2011 report, stated in part:

> And I think part of the GAO report as I read it was also saying maybe we need to recalculate getting fewer ships or whatever else. But what I don't have is people taking—giving us fewer missions. Our missions continue to increase so I remain committed to the original baseline of the eight national security cutters, the 25 OPCs and others [other systems] as they are in the projects [sic: POR?].[41]

Similarly, in commenting on a draft version of a September 2012 GAO report, the Coast Guard stated in part:

> The assets required to meet Coast Guard statutorily required missions do not change on the basis of budgetary constraints. While changes in the fiscal environment may impact the rate and efficiency at which the Coast Guard can acquire new cutters, aircraft, boats and C4ISR systems to replace aging and failing equipment, it does not reduce or otherwise change the needs of the Service.[42]

The September 2012 GAO report refers multiple times to a need for the Coast Guard, in managing its acquisition programs, to work within "realistic fiscal constraints" and "expected funding levels," which the report appears to define as an amount of acquisition funding level similar to the Coast Guard's FY2013 request and to the amounts that the Coast Guard received in

---

[39] Government Accountability Office, *Coast Guard[:]Action Needed As Approved Deepwater Program Remains Unachievable*, GAO-11-743, July 2011, summary page.

[40] See, for example, Government Accountability Office, *Coast Guard[:]Action Needed As Approved Deepwater Program Remains Unachievable*, GAO-11-743, July 2011, p. 46; and Government Accountability Office, *Observations on the Coast Guard's and the Department of Homeland Security's Fleet Studies*, GAO-12-751R, May 31, 2012.

[41] Source: Transcript of hearing.

[42] Letter dated September 13, 2012, from Jim H. Crumpacker, Director, [DHS] Departmental GAO-OIG Liaison Office, to John P. Hutton, Director, Acquisition Sourcing Management, U.S. Government Accountability Office, as reprinted in Government Accountability Office, *Coast Guard[:] Portfolio Management Approach Needed to Improve Major Acquisition Outcomes*, GAO-12-918, September 2012, p. 53.

the five years prior to FY2013.[43] Although the annual amounts of acquisition funding that the Coast Guard has received in recent years are one potential guide to what Coast Guard acquisition funding levels might or should be in coming years, there may be other potential guides. For example, one could envision potential guides that focus on whether Coast Guard funding for ship acquisition and sustainment is commensurate with Coast Guard funding for the personnel that in many cases will operate the ships. Observations that might be made in connection with this example include the following:

- The Coast Guard has about 12.9% as many active-duty personnel as the Navy.[44] If the amount of funding for surface ship acquisition and sustainment in the Coast Guard's budget were equivalent to 12.9% of the amount of funding in the Navy's shipbuilding account, it would be about $1.8 billion per year, or about 142% more than the $743.0 million that the Coast Guard is requesting for FY2014 for surface ship acquisition and sustainment programs.[45]

- Funding in the Navy's shipbuilding account is equivalent to about 51% of the Navy's funding for active-duty personnel.[46] If Coast Guard funding for surface ship acquisition and sustainment were equivalent to 51% of Coast Guard funding for military pay and allowances, it would be about $1.7 billion per year.[47]

It is not clear whether either of the two above observations would be appropriate as guides for determining appropriate levels of funding for Coast Guard surface ship acquisition and sustainment in coming years, or more appropriate than other guides. But it might also be argued that it is not clear that recent Coast Guard acquisition funding levels are the sole or most appropriate guide for determining appropriate levels of such funding in coming years, particularly since the Coast Guard has entered a period where it is seeking to replace multiple classes of assets. Although prior-year funding levels are often used in federal budgeting to determine what might be a realistic funding level for a program area for coming years, it might also be argued that a sole reliance on such a standard could short-circuit the policymaking process and limit options available to congressional (and executive branch) policymakers by in effect ruling out the option of deciding, as a matter of policy, that a program area is a high-enough priority that funding for it should be increased above prior-year levels, even while overall federal funding remains constrained. Supporters of this perspective might argue that what constitutes a realistic level of funding in coming years for a given program area is a policy question for congressional (and executive branch) policymakers to decide, and that an unvarying approach of basing future-year funding for various program areas on their prior-year funding levels would hamper the ability of the congressional (and executive branch) policymakers to alter the composition of the federal budget over time to meet changing federal needs.

---

[43] Government Accountability Office, *Coast Guard[:] Portfolio Management Approach Needed to Improve Major Acquisition Outcomes*, GAO-12-918, September 2012, p. 22-23, including Figure 7 on p. 23.

[44] The Coast Guard for FY2014 appears to be requesting an active-duty end strength—the number of active-duty military personnel—of 41,594 (measured by the Coast Guard in full-time equivalent [FTE] positions); the Navy for FY2014 is requesting an active-duty end strength of 323,600.

[45] The Navy's proposed FY2014 budget requests $14,078 million for the Shipbuilding and Conversion, Navy (SCN) appropriation account.

[46] The Navy's proposed FY2014 budget requests $27,824 million for the Military Personnel, Navy (MPN) appropriation account.

[47] The Coast Guard's proposed FY2014 budget requests $3,425.3 million for military pay and allowances.

At an October 4, 2011, hearing on the Coast Guard's major acquisition programs before the Coast Guard and Maritime Transportation subcommittee of the House Transportation and Infrastructure Committee, the following exchange occurred:

> REPRESENTATIVE FRANK LOBIONDO:
>
> Can you give us your take on what percentage of value must be invested each year to maintain current levels of effort and to allow the Coast Guard to fully carry out its missions?
>
> ADMIRAL ROBERT J. PAPP, COMMANDANT OF THE COAST GUARD:
>
> I think I can, Mr. Chairman. Actually, in discussions and looking at our budget—and I'll give you rough numbers here, what we do now is we have to live within the constraints that we've been averaging about $1.4 billion in acquisition money each year.
>
> If you look at our complete portfolio, the things that we'd like to do, when you look at the shore infrastructure that needs to be taken care of, when you look at renovating our smaller icebreakers and other ships and aircraft that we have, we've done some rough estimates that it would really take close to about $2.5 billion a year, if we were to do all the things that we would like to do to sustain our capital plant.
>
> So I'm just like any other head of any other agency here, as that the end of the day, we're given a top line and we have to make choices and tradeoffs and basically, my tradeoffs boil down to sustaining frontline operations balancing that, we're trying to recapitalize the Coast Guard and there's where the break is and where we have to define our spending.[48]

An April 18, 2012, blog entry stated:

> If the Coast Guard capital expenditure budget remains unchanged at less than $1.5 billion annually in the coming years, it will result in a service in possession of only 70 percent of the assets it possesses today, said Coast Guard Rear Adm. Mark Butt.
>
> Butt, who spoke April 17 [2012] at [a] panel [discussion] during the Navy League Sea Air Space conference in National Harbor, Md., echoed Coast Guard Commandant Robert Papp in stating that the service really needs around $2.5 billion annually for procurement.[49]

At a May 9, 2012, hearing on the Coast Guard's proposed FY2013 budget before the Homeland Security subcommittee of the Senate Appropriations Committee, Admiral Papp testified, "I've gone on record saying that I think the Coast Guard needs closer to $2 billion dollars a year [in acquisition funding] to recapitalize—[to] do proper recapitalization."[50]

---

[48] Source: Transcript of hearing.

[49] David Perera, "The Coast Guard Is Shrinking," *FierceHomelandSecurity.com*, April 18, 2012, accessed July 20, 2012, at http://www.fiercehomelandsecurity.com/story/coast-guard-shrinking/2012-04-18.

[50] Source: transcript of hearing. Papp may have been referring to remarks he made to the press before giving his annual state of the Coast Guard speech on February 23, 2012, in which reportedly stated that the Coast Guard would require about $2 billion per year in acquisition funding to fully replace its current assets. (See Adam Benson, "Coast Guard Cutbacks Will Cost 1,000 Jobs," *Norwich Bulletin*, February 23, 2012, accessed May 31, 2012, at http://www.norwichbulletin.com/news/x1138492141/Coast-Guard-cutbacks-will-cost-1-000-jobs#axzz1wSDAFCzX. See also "Coast Guard Leader Calls For More Ships," *MilitaryFeed.com*, February 24, 2012, accessed May 31, 2012, at http://militaryfeed.com/coast-guard-leader-calls-for-more-ships-5/; Associated Press, "Coast Guard Commandant Calls for New Ships," *TheLog.com*, March 10, 2012, accessed May 31, 2012, at http://www.thelog.com/SNW/Article/Coast-Guard-Commandant-Calls-for-New-Ships-to-Replace-Aging-Fleet; Mickey McCarter, "Congress Poised to Give Coast (continued...)

Potential oversight questions for Congress include the following:

- Under the POR force mix, how large a performance gap, precisely, would there be in each of the missions shown in **Table 6**? What impact would these performance gaps have on public safety, national security, and protection of living marine resources?

- How sensitive are these performance gaps to the way in which the Coast Guard translates its statutory missions into more precise statements of required mission performance?

- Given the performance gaps shown in **Table 6**, should planned numbers of Coast Guard cutters and aircraft be increased, or the Coast Guard's statutory missions reduced, or both?

- How much larger would the performance gaps in **Table 6** be if planned numbers of Coast Guard cutters and aircraft are reduced below the POR figures?

- Has the executive branch made sufficiently clear to Congress the difference between the number of ships and aircraft in the POR force and the number that would be needed to fully perform the Coast Guard's statutory missions in coming years? Why has public discussion of the POR focused mostly on the capability improvement it would produce over the legacy force, and rarely on the performance gaps it would have in the missions shown in **Table 6**?

- Why was the POR designed to fit within an originally estimated acquisition cost of about $24 billion? What analysis led to the selection of $24 billion as the appropriate total acquisition cost target for the POR?

- Are recent Coast Guard acquisition funding levels the sole or most appropriate guide in determining future Coast Guard acquisition funding levels? If recent Coast Guard acquisition funding levels are used as a guide in setting future Coast Guard acquisition funding levels, how would that affect Coast Guard ship and aircraft force levels, and consequently Coast Guard mission capability and capacity, over the long run?

NSC Program: No Funding Requested in FY2014 for Long Lead Time Materials (LLTM) for Eighth Ship

Another potential oversight issue for Congress is the lack of a request in the Coast Guard's proposed FY2014 budget for acquisition funding for long lead time materials (LLTM) to support the procurement of an eighth NSC in FY2015. Providing this funding—which might amount to about $77 million, based on the amount of LLTM funding provided in FY2012 for NSC 6— would improve the construction sequence for NSC 8 and thereby reduce its total acquisition cost by $30 million to $35 million, the Coast Guard estimates.[51]

(...continued)

Guard More Money Than Requested for FY 2013," *HSToday.us*, May 10, 2012, accessed May 31, 2012, at http://www.hstoday.us/focused-topics/customs-immigration/single-article-page/congress-poised-to-give-coast-guard-more-money-than-requested-for-fy-2013.html.)

[51] Source: Coast Guard briefing to CRS, June 14, 2013.

At an April 16, 2013, hearing on the Coast Guard's proposed FY2014 budget before the Homeland Security subcommittee of the House Appropriations Committee, the following exchange occurred:

> REPRESENTATIVE DAVID PRICE: Thank you. I'm certainly not inclined to question your commitment to the National Security Cutter number seven and giving that priority. Are we mistaken though to see the omission of the long lead time materials [for the eighth NSC] as a—as a setback or at least a—a—an omission that—that really is going to—if not throw number eight into doubt, at least greatly increases the [ship's] cost and the delay the timeframe [for building it].
>
> ADMIRAL ROBERT PAPP, COMMANDANT OF THE COAST GUARD: Now, there's no doubt that the omission of long lead money for number eight will increase the [ship's] cost. We had the same discussion last year and I was very grateful that the Subcommittee put in the long lead money for number seven. It helped us out greatly. It kept the project going. It's predictability for the shipyard and enables them to give us a better prices we negotiate [sic].
>
> And we have negotiated some very good prices on number six and I know we will on number seven. So it's a disappointment to me that we're unable to put the long lead for number eight in there but it's just one of those tough decisions I had to make based upon priorities on other projects that we have ongoing.[52]

Similarly, at an April 16, 2013, hearing before the Coast Guard and Maritime Transportation subcommittee of the House Transportation and Infrastructure Committee on the FY2014 budget for the Coast Guard and maritime transportation, Admiral Papp testified:

> So I'm grateful for the fact that we now have the money for National Security Cutter number seven in the budget. But that was helped quite frankly last year by both the House and the Senate, providing long lead money for number seven. Getting long lead money in the construction of the National Security Cutter saves us money in the long run, gives the shipyard predictability so they can—they can plan out economically and helps us in our negotiating position when we—when we work towards the contract on the next cutter.[53]

Similarly, at a May 14, 2013, hearing on the Coast Guard's proposed FY2014 budget before the Homeland Security subcommittee of the Senate Appropriations Committee, Admiral Papp testified:

> The—the wisdom of having [funding for] long lead materials is demonstrated though [the budget request for] this year. We had long lead materials for [NSC number] seven. In the F.Y. '12 budget, we were able to take that $30 million in cost avoidance and we actually worked that into our computations when we produced the '14 budget and the—and the level that we asked for to do the construction on number seven.
>
> So, that—that validation that long lead materials works, but I will take the money for the ship [i.e., NSC number eight] whatever way I can get it, and, right now, it's—it's with the full funding in next year's budget [i.e., FY2015].[54]

---

[52] Transcript of hearing.

[53] Transcript of hearing.

[54] Transcript of hearing.

FRC Program: FY2014 Request for Two (Rather than Six) Ships

Another potential oversight issue for Congress concerns the Coast Guard's FY2014 request for acquisition funding for two (rather than six) FRCs. At an April 16, 2013, hearing before the Coast Guard and Maritime Transportation subcommittee of the House Transportation and Infrastructure Committee on the FY2014 budget for the Coast Guard and maritime transportation, Admiral Robert Papp, the Commandant of the Coast Guard, stated the following when asked where the Coast Guard would apply any additional acquisition funding, above the Coast Guard's FY2014 request, that Congress might make available:

> Well, I'd be happy to address at least a large portion of that, sir. You know, first of all, last year when we sign up the capital improvement plan, there was no National Security Cutter number seven in it for the '14 budget, none for National Security Cutter number eight in a subsequent budget....
>
> After that, of course, the Fast Response Cutter. The shipyard is set up to construct six or receive orders for six Fast Response Cutters a year. We only had money for to the last year. We're grateful for the Congress, put money for four more so that we are potentially able to order six in fiscal year '13. But as the stance now, I only have enough money left within our (inaudible) accounts to offer up two.
>
> Next dollars I would spend would be on the Fast Response Cutter because ordering two per year, first of all is below the minimum quantity. We have to renegotiate the contract, which ultimately ends up in higher cost, building them in a slower rate and stretches out that program probably over the course of about 15 years at a much higher cost as our current patrol boat fleet is failing us rapidly and we're not getting the number of hours we need on them.
>
> So continuing the construction on the National Security Cutter and the Fast Response Cutters are my next highest priority.[55]

Similarly, at an April 16, 2013, hearing on the Coast Guard's proposed FY2014 budget before the Homeland Security subcommittee of the House Appropriations Committee, the following exchange occurred:

> REPRESENTATIVE JOHN CARTER (continuing): Let me ask a couple of questions about the Fast Response Cutter. Your FY '14 budget request includes just two Fast Response Cutters even though Congress denied the same short sighted—sort of short sighted proposal last year. We bailed out the flawed request and fully funded all six cutters. I guess that's maybe what some others anticipating they want us to do this year.
>
> As I understand it, by only requesting two cutters, you're squandering up to 30 million [dollars] in savings per year when compared to the procurement of six per year. Can you explain why you made this decision and you have to some extent already and do you plan to increase the procurement in our out-years so that we do not continue to squander savings and delay capability.
>
> The current requirements to patrol boat hours is 174,000 per year, but this budget supports less than half that requirement. Will we ever close the capability gap from what is funded to what is required for patrol boat hours, also what areas are most impacted by these gaps?

---

[55] Transcript of hearing.

ADMIRAL PAPP: Sir, I'd like to be maximizing our production of the Fast Response Cutter, I understand fully and I agree and I agree that it costs more when we don't order an economic order quantities.

Where our contract calls for a minimum order of four, maximum order of six, the shipyard is geared up to do six a year. They—they have to have some sort of consistency and predictability in terms of their production rate. But once again, this was one of those tough decisions that I face in the current fiscal environment putting in as many as I can while trying to keep other projects going and being focused on my highest priority.

Fast Response Cutter is one of my highest priorities. Now [sic: National] Security Cutter is my highest priority, so starting with that, I was only able to fit two Fast Response Cutters in. That gives us two options. We could renegotiate the contract to change the minimum order to two and as you recognized that ends up being a more expensive proposition.

In analyzing the FY '13 appropriation and the multi-year nature of the funding for those six, I believe we can spread out evenly an order of four in FY '13 and order—and take two of the funding for two and move that into FY '14 and do four per year. That's my second option at this point.[56]

Later in the hearing, when asked where the Coast Guard would apply would apply any additional acquisition funding, above the Coast Guard's FY2014 request, that Congress might make available, Admiral Papp replied:

Well, Sir, clearly, if there were additional funds, the first thing I would them to is the Fast Response Cutter. We absolutely need that boat. We—I acknowledge the patrol boat hour gap but the the hour gap is sort of species argument in my estimation because we assign so many hours per the number of hulls that we have out there. Frankly, some of those hulls particularly on the Island class are not able to do all the hours that they are supposed to do.

In fact, we have one [Island class] boat right now, the Chinkatig (ph) [sic: Chincoteague], which is laid up. It is—the hull is so deformed, we can't operate the ship. It would cost $3 million to get the ship back in condition so it could operate and that's just not money that's wisely spent. Yet, we've been unable to decommission any of the older patrol boats simply because we're trying to keep our numbers which then feed sort of—an artificial—artificial level of patrol boat hours that are out there.

What we really need are the hulls. And ultimately, we need to get all 58 of those fast response cutters built, not only because they performed the patrol boat mission but because they're also more capable ship. They interface with the Offshore Patrol Cutter which is our next big project and the National Security Cutter which ultimately give us fewer large ships in the offshore environment. But hopefully with a little bit more capability from these patrol boats, we'd be able to eliminate that gap.[57]

Similarly, at a May 14, 2013, hearing on the Coast Guard's proposed FY2014 budget before the Homeland Security subcommittee of the Senate Appropriations Committee, Admiral Papp testified:

---

[56] Transcript of hearing.

[57] Transcript of hearing.

The first option is to award those six [FRCs] in F.Y. '13, which was our original intent, and then renegotiate with the shipyard to see if we can go to a minimal order—[a] quantity of two for F.Y. '14.

We're at that point now where we can renegotiate. The fact of the matter is that renegotiating to build only two a year will increase the price. Our—our estimate [of the increase] is probably anywhere between $10 million and $20 million per ship. More when we go down to only two. Plus—plus it pushes out the replacement program to 18 years to get all those boats built. We'll be having to put the first one through a mid-life renovation before the last one is constructed.

So that's just the realities of what we're confronted with.

The other—the other option is to try and balance out [the procurement rate at] four [FRCs] per year [in FY2013 and FY2014] and I understand that's a little unfair to the ship builder, because they gear up, they bring people on board, they invest in their infrastructure based upon the—the prediction of six per year. And, as—as I've said in the past, we think if we build six a year our estimate is we get at least $30 million in cost avoidance.

I—I wanted to make sure that I was very clear and understood that, and I've had my people go back and take a look [as the estimated cost avoidance at a procurement rate of six per year]. I really think it's more than $30 million a year, but we start getting into competition sensitive information and things like that when we get any more detailed than that, but it's clear that when you use the economic order quantity, you will get those savings.[58]

As mentioned earlier (see "FRC Program" in "Background"), on September 25, 2013, the Coast Guard exercised an option for six FRCs (numbers 19-24 in the program).

FRC Program: Delays, Cost Growth, and Testing

Another potential oversight issue for Congress concerns delays, cost growth, and testing issues in the FRC program. A March 2012 report on the FRC program by Office of the Inspector General (OIG) of the Department of Homeland Security (DHS—the parent department of the Coast Guard) stated:

The Coast Guard's oversight of the Fast Response Cutter acquisition has helped ensure that the provisions of the contract reflect the Coast Guard's operational requirements and that the contractor is meeting the contract's provisions. However, the Coast Guard has executed an aggressive, schedule-driven strategy that allowed construction of the Fast Response Cutters to start before operational, design, and technical risks were resolved. Consequently, six cutters under construction required rework that resulted in at least 270 days of schedule delays for each cutter and a total cost increase of $6.9 million for the acquisition. This aggressive acquisition strategy also allowed the Coast Guard to procure 12 Fast Response Cutters before testing the lead cutter in actual operations. It is uncertain whether the Fast Response Cutter will perform as intended until it completes operational test and evaluation in actual maritime environments.

If operational test and evaluation on the lead Fast Response Cutter reveals deficiencies, the Fast Response Cutters may incur additional costly rework and delays, or the Coast Guard may have to accept Fast Response Cutters that do not fully meet its mission requirements.

---

[58] Transcript of hearing.

This may hinder the Coast Guard's ability to fill the critical shortages in its patrol boat fleet.[59]

The report also stated:

Recommendations

We recommend that the Assistant Commandant for Acquisitions, U.S. Coast Guard:

Recommendation #1: Ensure that future acquisitions employ a knowledge-based acquisition strategy to the maximum extent practicable by revising the U.S. Coast Guard's Major Systems Acquisition Manual to allow for a schedule-driven acquisition strategy to be employed only when it is properly authorized and supported by the results of a risk assessment and cost-benefit analysis.

Recommendation #2: Improve low-rate initial production decisions for the U.S. Coast Guard Surface Acquisition programs by issuing a policy memorandum that requires that it achieve a specific level of design maturity at Critical Design Review.

Recommendation #3: Issue a policy memorandum that requires authorization to proceed with low-rate initial production be supported by the reported results of operational assessments.

Recommendation #4: Revise the Coast Guard's acquisition policy to require a documented risk assessment when low-rate initial production quantity exceeds 10%, or other Coast Guard established minimum, of the total quantity approved for the acquisition.

Recommendation #5: Mitigate risk by executing plans for an operational assessment prior to delivery of the lead FRC and take immediate action to implement recommendations from the operational assessment. Any recommendations not implemented should be supported by the results of a risk assessment and cost-benefit analysis.[60]

The Coast Guard partially concurred with the first three recommendations and concurred with the final two.[61]

OPC Program: FY2014 Funding Request Less than Projected Under FY2013 Budget

Another potential oversight issue for Congress concerns the $25 million in acquisition funding requested for FY2014 for the OPC program. This figure is one-half of the $50 million that was projected for FY2014 under the Coast Guard's FY2013 budget submission. Compared to the FY2013 CIP, the FY2014 CIP in effect shifts $25 million in OPC acquisition funding from

---

[59] Department of Homeland Security, Office of Inspector General, *U.S. Coast Guard's Acquisition of the Sentinel Class – Fast Response Cutter*, OIG-12-68, March 2012, p. 1. Accessed June 29, 2012, at http://www.oig.dhs.gov/assets/ Mgmt/2012/OIG_12-68_Mar12.pdf. See also Calvin Biesecker, "Coast Guard's Aggressive Schedule On FRC Carries Technical Risks, IG Cautions," *Defense Daily*, April 13, 2012: 3-4.

[60] Department of Homeland Security, Office of Inspector General, *U.S. Coast Guard's Acquisition of the Sentinel Class – Fast Response Cutter*, OIG-12-68, March 2012, p. 13.

[61] Department of Homeland Security, Office of Inspector General, *U.S. Coast Guard's Acquisition of the Sentinel Class – Fast Response Cutter*, OIG-12-68, March 2012, pp. 14-17.

FY2014 to FY2015 (see **Table 3**). The Coast Guard states that this change in the funding profile reflects a refined estimate of the cost of the work to be done on the OPC program in FY2014 and FY2015, and does not change the program's schedule.[62]

OPC Program: Cost, Design, and Acquisition Strategy

Another potential oversight issue for Congress concerns the Coast Guard's acquisition strategy for the Offshore Patrol Cutter. Potential oversight questions for Congress include the following:

- Has the Coast Guard fully incorporated into the OPC acquisition strategy lessons learned from the NSC and FRC programs? What, in the Coast Guard's view, are those lessons?

- As mentioned earlier, the Coast Guard's RFP for the OPC program establishes an affordability requirement of an average unit price of $310 million per ship, or less, in then-year dollars for ships 4 through 9 in the program. How was the $310 million figure determined?

- What process is the Coast Guard using to evaluate tradeoffs in OPC performance features against this target construction price? What performance features have been reduced or eliminated to meet the target construction price?

- How much confidence does the Coast Guard have that the OPC that emerges from the tradeoff process could be built within the Coast Guard's target construction price?

- As mentioned earlier, the Coast Guard plans to award preliminary and contract design (P&CD) contracts as many as three competitors in FY2013. Is the number of potential P&CD contracts too high, too low, or about right? How did the Coast Guard arrive at this number?

- As also mentioned earlier, the Coast Guard plans to evaluate the P&CD efforts and then award one of the competitors a contract for detailed design development and ship construction. What process does the Coast Guard plan to use in evaluating the P&CD efforts? What evaluation factors does the Coast Guard plan to use, and how much weight will be assigned to each?

2012 Testimony

Some of the above questions have been discussed over the past two years at hearings on the Coast Guard's proposed FY2013 and FY2014 budgets. For example, at a March 6, 2012, hearing on the Coast Guard's proposed FY2013 budget before the Homeland Security Committee of the House Appropriations Committee, Admiral Robert J. Papp, Jr., the Commandant of the Coast Guard, stated:

> When I came in as commandant, I realized that this [the OPC program] was the most expensive project that the Coast Guard has ever taken on, honestly, as each [of the] 25 ships are a significant investment. And I also understood looking out at the horizon and seeing the

---

[62] Source: Coast Guard briefing to CRS, June 14, 2013.

storm clouds that restrict the budgets coming up there we needed to build a ship that was affordable.

We rescrubbed the requirements. We have battled ourselves within the Coast Guard to make sure we're asking for just exactly what we need, nothing more nothing less. And I have said three things to my staff as we go on forward—affordable, affordable, affordable.

And now I'm very pleased to say that just last week that the department [DHS] has reviewed—we passed a major milestone with acquisition decision event number two which validated our requirements for the type of cutter that we're looking for and we are ready to go towards the preliminary and contract design work this next year.[63]

Later in the hearing, the following exchange occurred:

ADERHOLT:

And there has been a discussion as to the capability of the OPC with objective design being more capable than the—than the threshold capability.[64] What is the current plan and capability of the OPC and what capability thresholds are you considering?

PAPP:

We—the driving one as I said is affordability, but having said that—and I'm not—I'm not trying to be funny here, but the—the sea-keeping capability being, you know, to operate in Sea State 5 is probably the most important to us right now because with fewer national security cutters, at least fewer than the hindrance posed that we have right now.

None of our medium endurance cutters—the 210 foot and 270 foot [medium-endurance] cutters that we have—can operate in the Gulf of Alaska and the Bering Sea and they do not have the long legs to be able to send them out in the—on some of the longer deployments that we do in the Pacific.

So it has to be able to launch the aircraft and boats in Sea State 5, you know, which is standard offset in the Bering Sea and also have endurance that we'll be able to keep it out there on station. And I believe it was 45 days [of operation at sea] we're looking for without refueling.[65]

---

[63] Source: Transcript of hearing.

[64] In the design of many U.S. weapon systems, *threshold* refers to a minimally acceptable level of capability, and *objective* refers to a higher (but also more expensive or technically challenging) level of capability.

[65] Source: Transcript of hearing. At a March 7, 2012, hearing on the proposed FY2013 budgets for the Coast Guard and maritime transportation programs before the Coast Guard and Maritime Transportation subcommittee of the House Transportation and Infrastructure Committee, the following similar exchange occurred:

REPRESENTATIVE LARSEN:

Admiral Papp, some questions about the offshore patrol cutter. Obviously, we're—we're a little bit (inaudible) before that's operational. And I have a question about whether or not the requirements for the OPC will prioritize one set of factors over a different set of factors. (inaudible) and Endurance, that might be more helpful in the Pacific versus speed, armament, and other requirements. How are you approaching the requirement—setting requirements to the OPC?

PAPP:

Sir, realizing that this is going to be the largest acquisition project that the Coast Guard has ever done and recognizing that these ships are going to last us 40 years, we're taking the law beyond this [sic: a long look at this?]. And I realize there are some people that feel like we have dragged our (continued...)

2013 Testimony

At an April 16, 2013, hearing before the Coast Guard and Maritime Transportation subcommittee of the House Transportation and Infrastructure Committee on the FY2014 budget for the Coast Guard and maritime transportation, the following exchange occurred:

> REPRESENTATIVE DON YOUNG: Admiral, I understand this morning you told the corporation you're going to reconsider the requirement for the Offshore Patrol Cutter and reopen the design competition; if that is correct, how long will this delay construction of much of the needy cutters, I mean, how long was—what will happen?
>
> ARMIRAL ROBERT PAPP, COMNMANDANT OF THE COAST GUARD: Sir, that wasn't quite an accurate report, I said that we remain committed to the Offshore Patrol Cutter and I was asked if the ability to operate in Sea State-5 was hard and fast and I said the highest requirement for the Offshore Patrol Cuter is affordability and as we evaluate the candidate vessels we may need to go back and look at some of the requirements, I'm hopeful that we don't have to.
>
> I think we hammered off these requirements, in fact reduce some of them when I came in as (inaudible) [sic: Commandant?] because I want to make sure this ship is affordable and I've reported to this subcommittee and other sub-committees that we are intent on making this an affordable ship for the Coast Guard.
>
> If we had opened it up to revise the see keeping capability there probably would be a delay but I have no intent to open that up at this point, we'd have to evaluate all the candidates that we have and I'm hopeful that we'll find three candidates that look affordable because we're going to need to operate this ship in Alaska and it's going to need to be able to launch and recover boats and aircraft while operating the barring sea.[66]

(...continued)

> feet a little bit or pushed this to the right a little bit, and I would say that's just not the case. It is a little delayed from where we started out.
>
> But when I came in as commandant, I realized that we were going to be facing constrained budgets. So I had the staff take a look at the OPC once again, scrub the requirements with a direction that the primary requirement is affordability. We just could not afford everything that was in the requirements before, so we set new thresholds for it.
>
> But the most important is the sea-keeping capability because with a reduced number of national security cutters, if we only have eight national security cutters replacing the 12 Hamilton class cutters, we have to have a ship that's capable of going up into the Gulf of Alaska, the Bering Sea, the Western Pacific.
>
> Our medium endurance cutters right now, and speaking as a captain of a 270-foot cutter, we cannot—those ships cannot perform in the extreme weather conditions that you find sometimes in the North Atlantic much less the Arctic, and the—the Bering Sea.
>
> So keeping the requirements for sea state five for helicopter launching and boat launching, and the Endurance were most important. And I'm really pleased to say that we have finally passed that hurdle. We went through acquisition decision event number two with the Department of Homeland Security last week, and they approved our requirements so we're—we're stepping out smartly now, moving ahead.
>
> (Transcript of hearing)

[66] Transcript of hearing.

Similarly, at an April 16, 2013, hearing on the Coast Guard's proposed FY2014 budget before the Homeland Security subcommittee of the House Appropriations Committee, the following exchange occurred:

> REPRESENTATIVE (UNKNOWN):[67] Thank you, Mr. Chairman. Admiral, there's been much discussion as to the capability of the OPC specifically the requirement to operate at sea state 5. Admiral, why is this requirement important? And if the current proposals come in too high, will you decrease the sea state requirement in order to meet the target price?
>
> ADMIRAL PAPP: I would not like to do that because that would probably delay the process, but we may have to recomplete the request for proposals by changing that standard. The reason we need the standard is because we'll have only eight National Security Cutters and while they are tremendously capable ships, they can't be in the same places as 12 high endurance cutters were that they are replacing.
>
> We've been comfortable with 12 high endurance cutters because that gave us enough to operate in the Bering Sea and in the Gulf of Alaska and the broad ranges of the—of the Pacific given the fact that we'll have fewer ships, in fact, we'll only have six National Security Cutters out on the West Coast because we need to keep two on the East Coast. We need to make sure that the offshore patrol cutters are capable of operating in Alaska.
>
> The 270-foot medium endurance cutters that we have were originally intended to be able to operate everywhere. We've tried to operate them in Alaska. You can't launch and recover boats and you can't launch and recover aircraft. They just aren't—cannot survive the sea state up there. And that is our—that is our world of work. We have to be able to launch boats for our boarding teams to go aboard fishing vessels. We need to be able to launch helicopters for search and rescue.
>
> So this requirement for sea state 5 has been our highest priority on that ship. I'm sorry. It's not been the highest priority. The highest priority has been affordability. And when people have asked me what are the three most important things about the offshore patrol cutter, I've constantly said, affordability, affordability, affordability. So that will be the driving factor on our down select for these three candidates and I'm hopeful that all three will not only be affordable but be able to survive in sea state 5—I'm sorry, not survive, but operate in sea state 5.[68]

September 2012 GAO Report

Regarding the Coast Guard's requirements development process for the OPC, a September 2012 GAO report states:

> **Coast Guard Took Positive Steps to Improve Requirements Development and Consider Affordability for the Offshore Patrol Cutter**
>
> The Coast Guard took some steps to improve the requirements development process for the Offshore Patrol Cutter—the largest acquisition in DHS's acquisitions portfolio and, according to officials, the first acquisition in the Deepwater surface fleet in which the Coast Guard had complete control over the requirements development process. The Coast Guard undertook studies and analysis that, in part, considered the measurability and testability as

---

[67] The transcript of the hearing shows the speaker as "unknown."

[68] Transcript of hearing.

---

required by guidance of the following four key performance parameters: operating range, operational sustainment and crew, speed, and patrol endurance. For example, the range requirement, which is the distance the cutter can travel between refueling, is clearly stated as a minimum acceptable requirement of 8,500 nautical miles at a constant speed of 14 knots to a maximum level of 9,500 nautical miles. Although cutters typically transit at various speeds over the course of a patrol, the Coast Guard conducted analysis to determine that the 14 knots speed at the minimum and maximum ranges would provide enough days between refueling given the percentage of time that the Coast Guard normally operates at certain speeds. By developing a measurable range requirement, the Coast Guard helped to promote a clear understanding of Offshore Patrol Cutter performance by potential shipbuilders and sought to balance the cost of additional range with the value that it provides. Furthermore, officials at the independent test authority—the Navy's Commander Operational Test and Evaluation Force—told us that they have been actively involved through the requirements development process and many of their questions regarding testability have been resolved.

Two other key performance parameters—seakeeping and interoperability—are not as consistent with the Coast Guard's guidelines of measurability and testability as identified in the Major Systems Acquisition Manual. For example the seakeeping key performance parameter described in the requirements document states that the Offshore Patrol Cutter shall be able to launch small boats and helicopters in 8.2- to 13.1-foot waves. However, in the specifications document, which is used to translate the requirements document into a level of detail from which contractors can develop a reasonably priced proposal, the Coast Guard states that the Offshore Patrol Cutter shall be able to launch small boats and helicopters in no more than 10.7 foot waves while transiting in a direction that minimizes the pitch and roll of the vessel—an important detail not specified in the requirements document. Further, the interoperability key performance parameter states that the Coast Guard must be able to exchange voice, video, and data with the Department of Defense and Homeland Security agencies. However, it does not list specific external partners or substantial details regarding the systems required to exchange data and the types and size of these data that could be examples of measurability and testability. This key performance parameter does not make this distinction between parts of the military that the Coast Guard operates with most often, such as the U.S. Navy and the intelligence community, and simply requires interoperability with all of DOD. Similarly, the interoperability key performance parameter does not specify the DHS agencies for which the Coast Guard must exchange data with, which makes this parameter difficult to test. Coast Guard's independent testing officials agreed that this key performance parameter, as currently written, is not testable in a meaningful way and stated that there are ongoing efforts to improve the clarity of this requirement.

During the requirements development process for the Offshore Patrol Cutter, the Coast Guard also made some decisions with respect to affordability. The following are examples where the Coast Guard made capability trades that are expected to help lower the program's acquisition cost:

- Speed—after a series of analyses, the Coast Guard decided to reduce the minimum acceptable speed from 25 to 22 knots thereby, according to officials, potentially eliminating the need for two diesel engines. According to a study completed by the Coast Guard, this trade could reduce the acquisition cost of each cutter by $10 million.

- Stern Launch—the Coast Guard removed the stern launch ramp capability from the Offshore Patrol Cutter design. While this trade-off may inhibit the launch and recovery of small boats in certain conditions, such as substantial roll or side-to-side movement of the vessel, Coast Guard officials stated that it will reduce the cost of the cutter because a stern launch ramp requires the cutter to be heavier, thus adding cost.

- C4ISR—the Coast Guard eliminated a minimum requirement for an integrated C4ISR system and instead is requiring a system built with interfaces to communicate between different software programs. According to Coast Guard officials, the Coast Guard now plans to use a Coast Guard-developed software system—Seawatch—rather than the more costly lead systems integrator-developed software system currently installed on the National Security Cutter, even though this system does not provide the Coast Guard with the capability to exchange near real-time battle data with DOD assets.

The improvements and affordability decisions that the Coast Guard has made in its requirements development process for the Offshore Patrol Cutter are even more evident when compared with the process for generating requirements for its other major cutter—the National Security Cutter. Due to the nature of the lead systems integrator strategy that the Coast Guard initially used to buy the National Security Cutter, Integrated Coast Guard Systems developed the requirements, designed, and began producing the National Security Cutter before the requirements document was completed. The Coast Guard did not have an operational requirements document at the time the Coast Guard awarded the construction contract for the first cutter in 2004, but the Coast Guard documented the requirements in 2006. Further, even as the third National Security Cutter was in production, Coast Guard was refining the requirements and, in January 2010, made the decision to clarify some key performance parameters such as anti-terrorism/force protection and underwater mine detection because the existing requirements were not testable. To further remedy the lack of clear requirements, Coast Guard officials stated that they are currently developing a second version of the requirements document that improves the specificity and definition of many of the National Security Cutter's requirements and will be used as criteria during operational testing. To date, the Coast Guard has not reduced the National Security Cutter's capability for the purpose of affordability as it has done for the Offshore Patrol Cutter. However, according to Coast Guard officials, there is a revised acquisition program baseline under review which will reflect an ongoing effort to lower the acquisition cost of the vessel.[69]

Regarding the potential accuracy of the Coast Guard's estimated procurement cost for the OPC, given the known procurement cost of the NSC, the September 2012 GAO report states:

> **Major Cutter Requirements and Missions Have Similarities, but Costs Vary Greatly and Concerns Remain about Affordability**
>
> The requirements and missions for the National Security Cutter and the Offshore Patrol Cutter programs have similarities, but the actual cost for one National Security Cutter compared to the estimated cost of one Offshore Patrol Cutter varies greatly. Even though the Coast Guard took steps to consider affordability while developing the requirements for the Offshore Patrol Cutter, those affordability decisions do not explain the magnitude in the difference between these two costs....
>
> This comparison raises questions whether the Offshore Patrol Cutter could be a less expensive, viable substitute for the National Security Cutter or whether there are assumptions built into the Offshore Patrol Cutter cost estimate, not related to requirements, which are driving the estimated costs down. With respect to the first, DHS, motivated by concerns about the affordability of the National Security Cutter program, completed a Cutter Study in August 2011 which included an analysis to examine the feasibility of varying the combination of objective—or optimal performing—Offshore Patrol Cutters and National Security Cutters in the program of record. Through this analysis, DHS found that defense

---

[69] Government Accountability Office, *Coast Guard[:] Portfolio Management Approach Needed to Improve Major Acquisition Outcomes*, GAO-12-918, September 2012, pp. 28-31.

operations is a key factor in determining the quantity of National Security Cutters needed and that the Coast Guard only needs 3.5 National Security Cutters per year to fully satisfy the planned requirement for defense-related missions. DHS concluded that with six National Security Cutters the Coast Guard can meet its goals for defense operations and mitigate some of the near-term capacity loss of the five National Security Cutter fleet modeled in the Cutter Study. DHS Program Analysis and Evaluation officials stated that this, in conjunction with other information, helped to inform the decision to not include the last two National Security Cutter hulls—hulls 7 and 8—in the fiscal years 2013-2017 capital investment plan. However, the DHS Cutter Study also notes that the time line for the two acquisitions makes a trade-off between the National Security Cutter and the Offshore Patrol Cutter difficult since the National Security Cutter program is in production whereas the Offshore Patrol Cutter program is only in the design phase. Similarly, we have reported that the Coast Guard may face an operational gap in its ability to perform missions using major cutters due to the condition of the legacy fleet.

With respect to the second possibility that there are assumptions built into the Offshore Patrol Cutter cost estimate that are driving the estimated costs down, the Coast Guard included three key assumptions in the Offshore Patrol Cutter's life cycle cost estimate, generally not related to the cutter's key requirements, which lower the estimated cost in comparison to the actual cost of the National Security Cutter. These three assumptions are:

- **Learning Curve.** The Coast Guard assumes that the shipyard(s) will generally continue to reduce the labor hours required to build the Offshore Patrol Cutter through the production of all 25 vessels. This may prove optimistic, particularly for later ships in the class, because the amount of additional learning per vessel–or efficiencies gained during production due to improving the manufacturing process to build the ship in a way that requires fewer labor hours–typically decreases over time in a shipbuilding program.

- **Military versus Commercial Standards.** The life cycle cost estimate assumes that certain areas of the Offshore Patrol Cutter's construction and material would reflect an average of 55 percent commercial standards—or construction standards that are typically used for military sealift ships that provide ocean transportation—and 45 percent military standards—or construction standards typically used for Navy combat vessels. Any changes in this assumption could have a significant effect on the cost estimate because military standards require more sophisticated construction applications, particularly in the areas of shock hardening and signature reduction, to prepare a ship to survive battle. Such sensitivity could help to explain the difference in costs between the Offshore Patrol Cutter program and the National Security Cutter program and officials stated that the latter program is being built to about 90 percent military standards.

- **Production Schedule.** The cost estimate reflects the Coast Guard's plan to switch from building one Offshore Patrol Cutter per year to building two Offshore Patrol Cutters per year beginning with the fourth and fifth vessel in the class. If the Coast Guard cannot achieve or maintain this build rate due to budget constraints, it may choose to stretch the schedule for the program which in turn could increase costs.

Coast Guard program officials generally agreed that these three variables are important to the cost of the Offshore Patrol Cutter and are key reasons why the Coast Guard expects one Offshore Patrol Cutter to cost less than half of one National Security Cutter. However, these officials recognized that the cost estimate for the Offshore Patrol Cutter is still uncertain since the cutter has yet to be designed—thus, the National Security Cutter's actual costs are more reliable. Coast Guard program officials also added that the cost estimate for the Offshore Patrol Cutter is optimistic in that it assumes that the cutter will be built in accordance with the current acquisition strategy and planned schedule. They noted that any delays, design issues, or contract oversight problems—all of which were experienced during the purchase of the National Security Cutter—could increase the eventual price of the Offshore Patrol Cutter.[70]

Multiyear Procurement (MYP)

Another potential oversight issue for Congress concerns the potential for using multiyear procurement (MYP), also known as multiyear contracting, in acquiring new cutters. With congressional approval, certain Department of Defense (DOD) programs for procuring ships, aircraft, and other items employ MYP as a way of reducing procurement costs. As part of its Navy's FY2013 budget submission, for example, the Navy requested (and Congress approved) authority for using MYP arrangements for DDG-51 destroyers to be procured in FY2013-FY2017, for Virginia-class submarines to be procured in FY2014-FY2018, and for V-22 Osprey tilt-rotor aircraft to be procured in FY2013-FY2017. Compared to the standard or default approach of annual contracting, MYP has the potential for reducing procurement costs by several percent.[71]

The statute that governs the use of MYP—10 U.S.C. 2306b—makes MYP available with congressional approval not only to DOD, but to other government departments, including DHS, the parent department of the Coast Guard.[72] Unlike the Navy and other DOD services, however, the Coast Guard is not using MYP for any of its ship or aircraft procurement programs.

A May 10, 2013, press report quotes Michael Petters, the CEO of Huntington Ingalls Industries (the builder of NSCs), as stating:

> We basically have proposed that if we really want to save some money, we should do multi-years on [the] National Security Cutter. We've not had any commitment to that from the Congress, and so those [contracts] are one ship at a time.[73]

Potential oversight questions for Congress include the following:

- Has the Coast Guard considered using MYP for procuring NSCs, OPCs, or FRCs? If not, why not?

- What would be the potential savings of using MYP for procuring the final two or three NSCs, for procuring OPCs, or for procuring FRCs?

- What are the potential risks or downsides of using MYP for procuring NSCs, OPCs, or FRCs?

---

[70] Government Accountability Office, *Coast Guard[:] Portfolio Management Approach Needed to Improve Major Acquisition Outcomes*, GAO-12-918, September 2012, pp. 31, 33-35.

[71] For more on MYP, see CRS Report R41909, *Multiyear Procurement (MYP) and Block Buy Contracting in Defense Acquisition: Background and Issues for Congress*, by Ronald O'Rourke and Moshe Schwartz.

[72] 10 U.S.C. 2306b(b)(2)(B).

[73] Michael Fabey, "HII: U.S. Non-Nuclear Shipbuilding Facing More Uncertainty Than Nuclear," *Aerospace Daily & Defense Report*, May 10, 2013: 4.

Alternative Force Mixes Equal in Cost to Program of Record

Another potential oversight issue for Congress is whether 8 NSCs, 25 OPCs, and 58 FRCs is the best mix of cutters that could be procured for the roughly the same total amount of acquisition funding. This issue was explored in a DHS Cutter Study that was completed in August 2011.[74] The study's synopsis states that

> In 2010, DHS was directed to conduct a study of USCG's major cutter recapitalization plan. The goal of this study was to evaluate whether an alternative cutter fleet mix could improve USCG's performance while maintaining current acquisition costs of the recapitalization program of record (POR). This question was motivated by the current fiscal environment and the increasing cost of the National Security Cutter (NSC), which in turn generated questions about its affordability and cost-effectiveness. However, the desired outcome was to provide insight into determining the most cost-effective fleet to execute USCG missions both near term and well into the future....

> The study was led by DHS Program Analysis and Evaluation (PA&E) with contract support from Center for Naval Analysis (CNA) and MicroSystems Integration (MSI)....

> The starting assumption for this study was that available USCG recapitalization funding is fixed at the cost of the POR. The study then identified and assessed the performance of alternative cutter fleets of equal acquisition cost, and compared the performance of these alternatives to the POR.[75]

The DHS Cutter Study examined force mixes that included not only NSCs, OPCs, and FRCs, but also two other ship-acquisition options—a modernized version of the Coast Guard's 270-foot Famous (WMEC-901) class medium-endurance cutter ("Mod-270" for short), and the Navy's Littoral Combat Ship (LCS).[76] (In recent years, some observers have suggested that the Coast Guard should procure the LCS in lieu of planned cutters, while other observers have suggested that the Navy should procure a modified version of the NSC in lieu of the LCS.) **Table 8** shows the nine alternative force mixes examined by the DHS Cutter Study, along with the POR mix.

---

[74] Alarik Fritz, Raymond Gelhaus, and Kent Nordstrom, *Options for the Future USCG Cutter Fleet, Performance Trade-Offs with Fixed Acquisition Cost*, IPR 14297, August 2011, 392 pp., accessed online October 23, 2012, at http://assets fiercemarkets net/public/sites/govit/dhscoastguardcutterstudy.pdf.

[75] Alarik Fritz, Raymond Gelhaus, and Kent Nordstrom, *Options for the Future USCG Cutter Fleet, Performance Trade-Offs with Fixed Acquisition Cost*, IPR 14297, August 2011, Synopsis of Results, p. 1.

[76] For more on the LCS program, see CRS Report RL33741, *Navy Littoral Combat Ship (LCS) Program: Background and Issues for Congress*, by Ronald O'Rourke.

Table 8. Alternative Force Mixes Examined in DHS Cutter Study

Ship type	POR	Group A			Group B			Group C		
		Fleet 1	Fleet 2	Fleet 3	Fleet 4	Fleet 5	Fleet 6	Fleet 7	Fleet 8	Fleet 9
NSC	8	5	7	9	5	7	8	8	8	8
OPC	25	30	26	23	0	0	0	22	19	16
Mod-270	0	0	0	0	41	37	34	0	0	0
LCS	0	0	0	0	0	0	0	3	6	9
FRC	58	58	62	59	60	58	58	58	58	58

Source: Alarik Fritz, Raymond Gelhaus, and Kent Nordstrom, *Options for the Future USCG Cutter Fleet, Performance Trade-Offs with Fixed Acquisition Cost*, IPR 14297, August 2011, p. 2

Regarding these alternative force mixes, the synopsis stated:

> Several alternative fleets were found to improve performance in certain missions and regions when compared to the POR. However, any improvements in mission performance over the POR came at a cost to mission performance in other areas. Thus, the study found that if DHS is willing to accept lower performance than the POR in selected missions and regions, it has two alternatives to the major cutter recapitalization POR:
>
> [Fleet 1]: Increase Offshore Patrol Cutter (OPC) fleet size in lieu of acquiring NSCs 6-8.
>
> [Fleet 6]: Increase OPC fleet size while selectively reducing OPC capability.[77]

The synopsis stated that exercising both of the above alternatives in tandem would lead to Fleet 4.[78] The synopsis stated that

> Both alternatives [Fleets 1 and 6] improve several end-state Coast Guard-wide measures of performance... without increasing USCG's major cutter acquisition costs. Moreover, these options are not mutually exclusive, and can be implemented in tandem. However, both alternatives require tradeoffs, and before selecting an alternative fleet recapitalization plan, DHS must determine whether the general performance benefits... are sufficient to offset these particular tradeoffs....
>
> Compared to the POR, the increased performance for these alternatives would likely not be seen, until the early 2030s, whereas some of the decreases in capability for [Fleet 1] would begin in 2018 and for [Fleet 6] by 2020. Also, [Fleet 1's] cumulative performance improvement will not meet and exceed the POR's until 2055....
>
> While the study did not model the performance of a six-NSC fleet, the near-term impacts were analyzed. Adding a sixth NSC to [Fleet 1] mitigates some of the near-term capacity loss when compared to the Program of Record, and mitigates some risk to performance of Defense Operations and Homeland Security Contingency response.

---

[77] Alarik Fritz, Raymond Gelhaus, and Kent Nordstrom, *Options for the Future USCG Cutter Fleet, Performance Trade-Offs with Fixed Acquisition Cost*, IPR 14297, August 2011, Synopsis of Results, pp. 1-2.

[78] Alarik Fritz, Raymond Gelhaus, and Kent Nordstrom, *Options for the Future USCG Cutter Fleet, Performance Trade-Offs with Fixed Acquisition Cost*, IPR 14297, August 2011, Synopsis of Results, p. 2.

This study also evaluated the potential for Navy's Littoral Combat Ship (LCS) to cost-effectively replace or augment the OPC fleet. An analysis of alternative cutter fleets that incorporated small numbers of LCS in the most favorable operating conditions showed that the LCS is not well-suited to USCG operations due to its limited range and ensuing inability to maintain effective presence. While the LCS has advanced capabilities, most notably its top-end speed, this does not offset its reduced presence. Therefore, based on acquisition costs used in this study, the OPC is clearly more cost-effective at executing USCG's major cutter mission set.[79]

GAO reviewed the DHS Cutter Study, as well as the Coast Guard's FMA Phase 1 and Phase 2 studies, and provided some observations on the three studies in a May 2012 report.[80] GAO states that "DHS PA&E and OMB [Office of Management and Budget] have so far used the Cutter Study to inform the fiscal year 2013 budget. For example, DHS PA&E officials stated that the Cutter Study provided information that DHS and OMB used, in conjunction with other information sources, to inform the decision to not include the last two NSC hulls—hulls 7 and 8—in the FY2013-2017 capital investment plan."[81] GAO further states that

> In the Cutter Study, the Center for Naval Analysis (CNA) recommends that DHS explore additional fleet mix options, including looking at a mid-capability OPC.
>
> The mid-capability OPC would reduce the speed and range of the objective OPC but otherwise maintain its presence capabilities including an ability to operate in sea state 5.
>
> A CNA official responsible for the analysis stated that other characteristics of this mid-capability OPC could include removing or reducing the following from the objective OPC without affecting presence:
>
> - Sensitive Compartmentalized Information Facility
>
> - Air Search and Fire Control Radars (acquire the positions of targets and provide these data to a ship's command and control and weapon systems)
>
> - Electronic Warfare Support Measures
>
> - Berthing space (114 instead of 122)
>
> - Weapons suite (e.g., 25mm gun instead of 57mm)
>
> The CNA official also stated that CNA has not studied whether these changes to the objective OPC would otherwise affect mission performance.[82]

Potential oversight questions for Congress include the following:

---

[79] Alarik Fritz, Raymond Gelhaus, and Kent Nordstrom, *Options for the Future USCG Cutter Fleet, Performance Trade-Offs with Fixed Acquisition Cost*, IPR 14297, August 2011, Synopsis of Results, pp. 2-3.

[80] Government Accountability Office, *Observations on the Coast Guard's and the Department of Homeland Security's Fleet Studies*, GAO-12-751R, May 31, 2012.

[81] Government Accountability Office, *Observations on the Coast Guard's and the Department of Homeland Security's Fleet Studies*, GAO-12-751R, May 31, 2012, p. 3.

[82] Government Accountability Office, *Observations on the Coast Guard's and the Department of Homeland Security's Fleet Studies*, GAO-12-751R, May 31, 2012, briefing slide 18.

- What role, exactly, did the DHS Cutter Study play in the executive branch decision to not include funding for the seventh and eighth NSC in the Coast Guard's FY2013 five-year capital investment plan? Does the DHS Cutter Study provide a sufficient analytical basis for such a decision?

- Is the Coast Guard's currently planned mix of 8 NSCs, 25 OPCs, and 58 FRCs the best mix of cutters that could be procured for the roughly the same amount of acquisition funding? What were the conclusions of the DHS Cutter Study regarding the levels of overall mission effectiveness of the nine alternative forces mixes relative to one another, and to the POR mix?

- What is the Coast Guard's assessment of the option of developing and procuring a modified version of the 270-foot Famous-class medium-endurance cutter?

- What is the Coast Guard's assessment of the option suggested by the CNA official for acquiring a "mid-capability OPC" as described in the GAO report?

Information for Supporting Congressional Oversight of Procurement Programs

Another oversight issue for Congress concerns the adequacy of information available to Congress to support review and oversight of Coast Guard procurement programs, including cutter procurement programs. The Coast Guard has entered a period where, like the Navy, it is requesting significant funding each year from Congress to execute multiple ship procurement and modernization programs. Congress, however, lacks ready access to basic information exhibits on Coast Guard shipbuilding programs that are equivalent to those that support congressional review and oversight of Navy ship procurement programs.

Basic information exhibits readily available to Congress that support congressional review and oversight of Navy ship procurement programs include but are not limited to the following:

- annual **Budget Item Justification Sheets (P-40 Exhibits)**, **Weapon System Cost Analysis sheets (P-5 Exhibits)**, and **Ship Production Schedules (P-27 Exhibits)** for each Navy shipbuilding program—exhibits that present detailed information on year-to-year program funding, unit procurement costs, and production schedules (see **Appendix B** for examples);

- annual **Selected Acquisition Reports (SARs)** that DOD prepares for major DOD acquisition programs, which present supplementary data on program cost estimates, annual funding, and contract;

- a concise statement of the Navy's **ship force structure goal**—the Navy's current force structure goal is to achieve and maintain a fleet of about 310-316 battle force ships, consisting of certain types and numbers of ships (see **Appendix C**);

- an annual **five-year Navy shipbuilding plan** that shows planned annual procurement quantities for each type of ship being procured (see **Appendix D**); and

- an annual **30-year Navy shipbuilding plan** that shows annual procurement quantities and projected Navy ship force levels over the next 30 years (see **Appendix E**).

These information exhibits assist Congress in doing the following, among other things, in reviewing and conducting oversight on Navy shipbuilding programs:

- identifying and evaluating cost growth and schedule delays in the execution of shipbuilding programs;

- understanding the relationship between annual procurement rates and unit procurement cost;

- evaluating whether programs are achieving satisfactory production learning curves over time;

- evaluating whether proposed sequences of annual procurement quantities for programs would be efficient to execute from an industrial standpoint;

- evaluating stability in Navy shipbuilding planning by tracking year-to-year changes in the five-year shipbuilding plan;

- identifying potential financial and industrial-base linkages between shipbuilding programs that are being funded in overlapping years;

- identifying and evaluating Navy assumptions concerning service lives and retirement dates for existing ships;

- evaluating whether ship procurement needs are being pushed into the future, potentially creating an expensive ship procurement "bow wave" in coming years; and

- understanding when the Navy will achieve its ship force level goals, and whether the Navy will experience ship inventory shortfalls relative to those goals that could affect the Navy's ability to perform its missions in coming years.

Although the Coast Guard and the Department of Homeland Security submit substantial budget-related information to Congress each year, Congress lacks ready access to the five sources of detailed program information listed above:

- Although the Coast Guard's annual budget submission includes a budget-justification book,[83] the entries in that book for the Coast Guard's ship procurement programs do not present information as detailed and structured as that presented in the P-40, P-5, and P-27 exhibits.

- Reports on Coast Guard programs equivalent to DOD's SAR reports are not readily available to Congress.

- The Coast Guard's POR is a statement of desired procurement quantities for certain procurement programs, but not a concise statement of the Coast Guard's overall ship force structure objective, which would take into account continued service of existing ships that are not in need of immediate replacement.

- The Coast Guard's five-year capital investment plan shows annual funding amounts for individual programs, but not annual procurement quantities, and

---

[83] For the FY2013 budget, this is *Department of Homeland Security, United States Coast Guard, Fiscal Year 2012 Congressional Justification*, 400 pp.

annual procurement quantities are not always easy to discern from annual funding amounts.

- The Coast Guard's budget submission does not include an equivalent of the Navy's 30-year shipbuilding plan.

A lack of ready access to these five sources of detailed program information can make it more difficult for Congress to conduct similar evaluations of Coast Guard programs. As a consequence, programs might, for example, be more likely to be reviewed over shorter time horizons, or in isolation from one another.

A potential issue for Congress is whether to require the Coast Guard and the Department of Homeland Security to provide equivalents to some or all of the five information sources listed above. Opponents of this option might argue that the Coast Guard and DHS already provide substantial budget-justification information to Congress, and that preparing Coast Guard equivalents to some or all of these five information sources would be an expensive and time-consuming proposition. Supporters of this option might argue that the cost of preparing and submitting this information would be small relative to the combined total acquisition cost the NSC, OPC, and FRC programs, and that information of this kind has proven to be of value in supporting congressional review and oversight of Navy shipbuilding programs.

Legislative Activity for FY2014

Summary of Appropriations Action on FY2014 Acquisition Funding Request

Table 9 summarizes appropriations action on the Coast Guard's request for FY2014 acquisition funding for the NSC, OPC, and FRC programs.

Table 9. Summary of Appropriations Action on FY2014 Acquisition Funding Request

Figures in millions of dollars, rounded to nearest tenth

Request	Request	House Appropriations Committee	Senate Appropriations Committee	Conference
NSC program	616	603.6[a]	632[b]	
OPC program	25	25	25	
FRC program	75	205[c]	310[d]	
TOTAL	716	833.6	967	

Source: For House Appropriations Committee: H.Rept. 113-91 of May 29, 2013, p. 71; for Senate Appropriations Committee: S.Rept. 113-77 of July 18, 2013, p. 84.

a. The exact figure is $603.553 million. Within this total, $77 million is to be used for long lead time materials (LLTM) for NSC 8.

b. Within this total, $77 million is to be used for long lead time materials (LLTM) for NSC 8.

c. Recommended increase of $130 million is for two additional FRCs.

d. Recommended increase of $235 million is for four additional FRCs.

FY2014 DHS Appropriations Act (H.R. 2217)

House

In addition to recommending the funding amounts shown in **Table 9**, the House Appropriations Committee states the following in its report (H.Rept. 113-91 of May 29, 2013) on H.R. 2217:

> The President's fiscal year 2014 budget for DHS's fiscal year 2014 proposes to [among other things]:
>
> • Reduce Coast Guard staffing by—850 military personnel; [and]...
>
> • Reduce the Coast Guard's recapitalization and acquisitions by—40 percent;....
>
> Beyond these proposed reductions, further analysis reveals that the President's fiscal year 2014 budget request for DHS will have the following performance impacts [among others]:
>
> • The lowest level of drug interdiction effectiveness in the past five years; [and]
>
> • A complete inability of the Coast Guard to fulfill its patrol boat mission requirements;...
>
> In short, the fiscal year 2014 budget request for DHS proposes to not only reduce the immediate resources of the Department's most critical frontline components, it proposes to substantially diminish the long-term security capabilities of our Nation.
>
> The Committee categorically rejects this flawed budget request for DHS.
>
> ... the bill [as reported] supports essential security operations by [among other things]:
>
> • Restoring nearly all of the proposed reductions to the Coast Guard's operating and acquisition budgets and increases funding for counternarcotics operations and sustainment of aging assets;... (Pages 4-5)

The report also states:

> Over the last several years, the Department has continually requested a substantial reduction in funding that would degrade the Coast Guard's operational capabilities and military workforce without proposing a compensatory proposal to rebuild the depleted capacity in the long term by investing in recapitalized assets. Those proposals had obvious, adverse implications for the Coast Guard's critical statutory missions of maritime safety, coastal security, and drug interdiction; ignored current threat activity and the ramifications for the Department's broader security and response efforts; and were resoundingly rejected by Congress.
>
> The fiscal year 2014 proposal is even more egregious, and gives the impression that this Administration does not appropriately value the work of the Coast Guard. It includes the lowest level of drug interdiction effectiveness in the past five years and reduces recapitalization funding to unsustainable levels. Over the past decade when our Nation has called for help, the Coast Guard has responded: they responded on the morning of 9/11 by helping untold numbers of people evacuate the devastation of lower Manhattan; they responded during the aftermath of Katrina by saving survivors stranded on rooftops; they responded by being the first to arrive in Haiti after an earthquake hit the country and killed thousands; and more recently, they responded to the worst oil spill in the history of our

Nation. If the country intends for the Coast Guard of tomorrow to be as effective as the Coast Guard we have today, and have depended on for decades, these reductions must be resoundingly rejected. Within the recommendation, the Committee has made targeted increases to address the inadequacy of the Department's request—adding capacity to the Coast Guard for today and for tomorrow. (Pages 66-67)

The report also states:

Mission Needs Statement

No Administration has ever proposed a budget that begins to close the mission hour gap the Coast Guard created on paper when it rebaselined its acquisition programs after 9/11. As highlighted by the GAO, the Coast Guard acquisition program is unachievable—particularly if the Coast Guard will be limited to a Capital Investment Plan (CIP) that is less than $1,000,000,000 per year for the next five years as is provided in the current plan. The Coast Guard's acquisition budget has grown dramatically in the years since 9/11, but, particularly in light of the steep and dramatic cuts proposed in this year's CIP, there is no reason to believe the gaping space between the 1998 baseline and the 2004 baseline will ever close in any significant way for aircraft or patrol boats. The mission hour target dropped for major cutters in the 2004 rebaselining, but remains unattainable through 2030 since it appears to assume the production of two Offshore Patrol Cutters (OPC) per year. However, even if the OPC currently under source selection meets the requirements laid out in the Coast Guard's Operational Requirements Document, it seems unlikely at the levels included in the CIP that such a program would be sustainable. Therefore, the Committee directs the Coast Guard to begin the process of developing a new mission needs statement that takes into account today's fiscal environment. If the Administration truly plans for the Coast Guard funding level to be what was presented in the Fiscal Year 2014 CIP, then this process should also address what missions the Coast Guard will no longer be able to achieve. The Committee notes that in the Fiscal Year 2014 Coast Guard Budget Hearing, the Commandant commented that the patrol boat hour requirement was "specious". The Committee cannot continue to accept a requirements document that is doubted by the senior leader of the Coast Guard. In order to plan for the future, the Coast Guard must match requirements to resources and provide an achievable plan. (Pages 67-68)

Regarding the Coast Guard's Acquisition, Construction, and Improvements (AC&I) account, the report states:

The Committee recommends significant restructuring of numerous programs to align funding with the requirements in the fiscal year of need.[84] Further, the recommendation provides funding for programs that have a proven track record, are low risk, have known costs, and provide increased capability. The Committee recommends a net reduction of $12,447,000 requested for the National Security Cutter (NSC)....

The Committee recommends the following increases [among others] above the amount requested: an increase of $130,000,000 above the amount requested for two additional FRCs; ... and an increase of $77,000,000 for long lead time materials for NSC 8. (Pages 70 and 71)

The funding table on page 71 of the committee's report shows a total of $603.553 million for the NSC program, reflecting the above-mentioned net reduction of $12.447 million from the Coast Guard's request. The implication is that the $77 million in funding for LLTM for NSC 8 is not in

---

[84] The report similarly states on page 7 that "The Committee continues to press reform of inefficient budgeting for Coast Guard acquisitions by aligning funding to requirements based on the fiscal year of need."

addition to, but rather forms part of, the total recommended appropriation for the NSC program of $603.553 million. This appears to be confirmed by another passage from the committee's report, which states:

National Security Cutter

The Committee recommends $603,553,000 for the NSC program to include long lead time material for NSC 8, $12,447,000 below the amount requested and $75,068,000 below the amount provided in fiscal year 2013. The recommendation includes a decrease of $12,447,000 for contract savings associated with the contract for the sixth NSC. The recommendation also defers funding for post-delivery activities that are requested unnecessarily ahead of need.

Fast Response Cutter

The Committee recommends $205,000,000 for the acquisition of four FRCs, $130,000,000 above the amount requested and $129,665,000 below the amount provided in fiscal year 2013. The fiscal year 2014 budget request included funding for only two FRCs. This represents almost $30,000,000 in savings that will not be realized and delays the delivery of much needed capability. This is the same type of budget gimmickry the Department proposed and Congress rejected in fiscal year 2013. It is unclear as to how the Department plans to close the various gaps in needed capability if it continues to make such ineffective and unjustified budget requests. (Page 73)

The section of H.R. 2217 as reported that appropriates funds for the Coast Guard's Acquisition, Construction, and Improvements (AC&I) account includes several provisos, including the following:

... *Provided*, That the funds provided by this Act shall be immediately available and allotted to contract for the production of the seventh National Security Cutter notwithstanding the availability of funds for post-production costs: *Provided further*, That the funds provided by this Act shall be immediately available and allotted to contract for long lead time materials, components, and designs for the eighth National Security Cutter notwithstanding the availability of funds for production costs or post-production costs:...

Section 516 of the bill as reported states:

Sec. 516. Any funds appropriated to Coast Guard 'Acquisition, Construction, and Improvements' for fiscal years 2002, 2003, 2004, 2005, and 2006 for the 110-123 foot patrol boat conversion[85] that are recovered, collected, or otherwise received as the result of negotiation, mediation, or litigation, shall be available until expended for the Fast Response Cutter program.

Section 568 of the bill as reported rescinds certain prior-year Coast Guard Acquisition, Construction, and Improvement (AC&I) account funding. Regarding these rescissions, the committee's report states:

The Committee recommends the following rescissions [among others] in Title V of this bill [**Section 568** as reported] from prior year accounts:... from funds provided in fiscal year

---

[85] This is a reference to a canceled Coast Guard program to modernize the Coast Guard's 110-foot Island class patrol boats with a work package that would, among other things, lengthen the boats to 123 feet.

2011,... $12,612,000 for excessive antecedent liability and economic price adjustment funding in the Fast Response Cutter (FRC) program; from funds provided in fiscal year 2012,... $29,500,000 from funds for the FRC to include $22,500,000 for excessive antecedent liability and economic price adjustment funding; and from funds provided in fiscal year 2013, $22,000,000 for excessive antecedent liability and economic price adjustment funding in the FRC program, $10,480,000 from the NSC program to include $5,000,000 for a post shakedown availability for NSC 4, $1,882,000 for a gantry crane and davit for NSC 6, and $3,598,000 for waterfront changes associated with NSC 6. (Page 71)

The committee's report also states:

Full Funding

The Committee included a new general provision in fiscal year 2013 to address the lack of clarity in certain programs with respect to budgeting for long lead-time materials, end items, outfitting, post-delivery activities, spares, program management, and contract closeout. However, it is clear that the Department has chosen to ignore that direction based on this year's request for the NSC. Similar to the fiscal year 2013 request, the fiscal year 2014 request for the NSC includes funding for post-delivery activities of the seventh NSC that will not occur until fiscal year 2019 and does not request funding for the long lead time materials for NSC 8, even though the Department plans to procure an eighth NSC in fiscal year 2015.

Section 557 of Public Law 113–6 specifically addressed these issues by mandating the Department develop a fiscal policy that prescribes budgetary policies, procedures, and technical direction necessary to comply with the section's definitions of full funding. To further address this issue, the Committee includes a new provision in Title V of this bill [**Section 548** as reported] directing the Department to provide a report with the submission of the President's fiscal year 2015 budget that details its compliance with section 557 of Public Law 113–6. (Pages 72-73)

Senate

In addition to recommending the funding amounts shown in **Table 9**, the Senate Appropriations Committee states the following in its report (S.Rept. 113-77 of July 18, 2013) on H.R. 2217:

NATIONAL SECURITY CUTTER

The Coast Guard operates a fleet of 378-foot high endurance cutters [HECs] that are over 43 years old on average, and are increasingly unreliable and expensive to maintain. By comparison, the average Navy ship is 20 years old. The Coast Guard's program of record is to acquire 8 national security cutters [NSCs] to replace 12 HECs (of which 3 have been decommissioned with the arrival of the first 3 NSCs). To date, approximately $3,848,000,000 has been appropriated for six NSCs and long lead time materials [LLTM] for NSC–7. Three NSCs have been delivered to the Coast Guard, the fourth is expected to be delivered in fiscal year 2014, the fifth in fiscal year 2015, and the sixth in 2017.

As noted in prior years, the Committee strongly supports the procurement of one national security cutter per year until all eight planned ships are procured. The continuation of production without a break will ensure that these ships, which are vital to the Coast Guard's mission, are procured at the lowest cost, and that they enter the Coast Guard fleet as soon as possible. The Committee is concerned that the Administration's current acquisition policy requires the Coast Guard to attain total acquisition cost for a vessel, including long lead time materials, production costs, and post-production costs, before a production contract can be awarded. This has the potential to create shipbuilding inefficiencies, force delayed obligation of production funds, and require postproduction funds far in advance of when they will be used. As an example of such inefficiency, the fiscal year 2013 budget request proposed a rescission and reappropriation of $25,000,000 in funds previously appropriated for NSC–4 post-production that would have expired before they could be spent. The Department should be in a position to acquire NSCs in the most efficient manner within the guidelines of strict governance measures. Therefore, the Committee includes language in the bill specifying that funds made available by this act shall be available to contract for long lead time materials for Coast Guard vessels, notwithstanding the availability of funds for production costs or post-production costs.

For NSC–7, the Committee includes $12,000,000 for Segment 2 of LLTM. The Committee recommendation also includes $540,000,000, as requested, for production and $3,000,000 for postproduction costs. Funding for post-production costs is $61,000,000 below the request due to the fact that these funds are not necessary until fiscal years 2016 through 2018.

The request includes no funding for LLTM for NSC–8. The Committee disagrees with this proposal. Procuring these materials in advance will save substantial time and money by ensuring that supplies and components that require a long time to obtain are available to the manufacturer when they are needed. By providing LLTM for NSC–6 in advance, the Coast Guard was able to save $30,000,000 in the total cost of the ship. Therefore the bill includes $77,000,000 for LLTM for NSC–8. According to the Department, this will accelerate the production schedule for the cutter and result in direct savings of up to $40,000,000 compared to delaying long lead acquisition to fiscal year 2015.

FAST RESPONSE CUTTER

The Committee recommends $310,000,000 for the Coast Guard's Fast Response Cutter [FRC]. This funding will allow the Coast Guard to acquire six FRC hulls (25–30). Procuring six FRCs in fiscal year 2014 will maximize the production line and generate cost savings of at least $5,000,000 per hull for a total savings to the taxpayers of $30,000,000. Funding six boats instead of two will also allow the Coast Guard to advance the replacement of the aging 110-foot island class patrol boats, which are already beyond the end of their projected service lives and very expensive to maintain. Each FRC will provide 2,500 annual operating hours and improved sea keeping ability, resulting in better habitability and full-mission capability in higher sea states.

OFFSHORE PATROL CUTTER

The recommendation includes $25,000,000 for the Offshore Patrol Cutter [OPC], as requested. Funding is provided for pre-acquisition design work of the OPC, which is intended to replace the Coast Guard's aging fleet of medium endurance cutters. The Coast Guard expects to award preliminary and contract designs to three competing contractors in fiscal year 2013. A final detailed design and construction award is expected in fiscal year 2016.

The OPC's initial capabilities to control and direct aircraft as well as execute interdiction missions should, to the maximum extent feasible, be equivalent to that of the NSC to facilitate maximum savings to the Federal Government, rather than being deferred to future upgrades that add to total cost of ownership. The Committee urges the Coast Guard to maximize, to the greatest extent practicable, such systems' commonality between the OPC and the NSC to reduce total acquisition cost and lifecycle costs facilitated by savings in life cycle logistics management, integration costs, and personnel training efficiencies. (Pages 87-88; material in brackets as in original)

The report also states:

COMMITTEE RECOMMENDATIONS

The President's fiscal year 2014 discretionary budget request proposes to reduce funding for the Coast Guard by 8 percent, including the reduction of over 850 military billets, the movement of 1,050 reservists to inactive status resulting in the smallest reserve force since 1957, the decommissioning of critical operational assets, and a 38 percent reduction in capital expenditures to a level not seen since 2003. When testifying before the subcommittee on the fiscal year 2014 budget request, the Commandant of the Coast Guard said that the proposed budget reductions could cause a "death spiral", as the agency would be forced to sustain cutters that average over 46 years of age instead of having funding to procure new vessels and aircraft. If the budget request were to be enacted, the Coast Guard's ability to carry out its 11 statutory missions would be seriously hampered. The recommended level provided for in this bill includes targeted increases above the President's request to ensure that Coast Guard personnel serving on the front lines have the resources and assets to fulfill their many missions in fiscal year 2014 and in the future. (Pages 73-74)

The report also states:

OPERATIONAL ENHANCEMENTS

High Endurance Cutters.—The budget request proposes to decommission two high endurance cutters [HECs] and 368 associated billets. These cutters average 46 years in age and have become increasingly unreliable. The Committee, however, is concerned that the decommissioning of two cutters in fiscal year 2014 would result in a significant cutter hour gap before new National Security Cutters [NSCs] are delivered to replace them. To date, four HECs have been decommissioned and the Coast Guard has delivered three NSCs. The fourth NSC is under production and scheduled for delivery in late fiscal year 2014 and the fifth NSC is under contract and scheduled for delivery in fiscal year 2015. Historically, HECs provide the greatest resource hour contribution to the counterdrug mission, both in the Eastern Pacific and Western Hemisphere. In fiscal year 2012, the Coast Guard seized 107 metric tons of cocaine, more than all other Federal agencies combined. The proposed reduction of two HECs with only one national security cutter delivered in fiscal year 2014 will result in a diminished presence and fewer opportunities for interdictions. Therefore, the recommendation includes an additional $8,000,000 and 184 positions to maintain one of the two HECs proposed to be decommissioned in the request, saving 1,665 major cutter hours (3,330 hours annualized) that otherwise would have been cut. (Page 76; material in brackets as in original)

The report also states:

LEGACY PATROL BOATS

A total of six fast response cutters [FRCs] are funded within the "Acquisition, Construction, and Improvements" appropriation, four boats and $235,000,000 above the request. This will bring the total amount funded to 30 boats, 12 of which will be in-service by the end of 2014. FRCs are replacing aging 110-foot Island Class Patrol Boats, which are already beyond the end of their projected service lives and very expensive to maintain. The Committee has learned that two of these patrol boats have such severe hull deterioration, it has become cost prohibitive to maintain them beyond fiscal year 2013. Given the fact that the bill increases the number of new patrol boats by four, providing for 10,000 additional operational hours, the Committee expects the Coast Guard to decommission two legacy patrol boats that are in the worst material condition, achieving savings of $2,763,000. (Page 80; material in brackets as in original)

The report also states:

INFRASTRUCTURE AND RESPONSE CAPABILITIES IN THE ARCTIC

The Committee is concerned about the lack of assets available for the Coast Guard's Arctic mission. No later than 120 days after the date of enactment of this act, the Commandant is directed to submit a report to the Committee comparing the costs of facility renovations to homeport and support an NSC in Alaska with the annual costs of transit time to Alaska area of operations for deployments and days lost to casualty repairs. (Pages 80-81)

The report also states:

ACQUISITION PORTFOLIO REVIEW

The fiscal year 2014 CIP [Five Year Capital Investment Plan] that was submitted to the Committee on April 19, 2013, calls for a radical change to Coast Guard recapitalization efforts in future years. The funding levels suggested in the plan would decrease the number of fast response cutters to a level that jeopardizes the program, stop the acquisition of new aircraft, delay completion of the offshore patrol cutter, put the acquisition of a new polar icebreaker at risk, and scale back investment in deteriorating shore facilities. If enacted, this investment plan would have dire consequences on the Coast Guard's ability to carry out its missions, such as: interdicting drugs in the transit zone; managing a mass migration event; responding to oil spills; fisheries enforcement; and the need to increase U.S. presence in the Arctic. The CIP states that DHS will conduct a comprehensive portfolio review in 2013 that will help develop revised acquisition program baselines and direct key acquisition decision events to reflect acquisition priorities and operational requirements achievable within the funding projections contained in the fiscal year 2014 CIP. A major flaw in the fiscal year 2014 CIP is the Department's conclusion that the funding levels it contains for the "Acquisition, Construction, and Improvements" appropriation are consistent with the presequester caps imposed on discretionary budget authority through 2021 under the Budget Control Act of 2011. The reality is that the fiscal year 2014 budget request for the "Acquisition, Construction, and Improvements" appropriation is 38 percent below the fiscal year 2013 enacted level, after factoring out emergency supplemental funding, while total discretionary spending under the Budget Control Act of 2011 increases by 1.4 percent between fiscal year 2013 and fiscal year 2014. In conducting the portfolio review described in the CIP, the Department shall use more appropriate outyear funding levels that are reflective of the fiscal year 2013 enacted level for the "Acquisition, Construction, and Improvements" appropriation, as adjusted by the pre-sequester caps set in the Budget Control Act of 2011. Finally, the review is to include acquisition cost, asset capability and quantity tradeoffs, and the overall impact to the Coast Guard's ability to carry out all of its statutory missions. The results of the review shall be validated by an independent third party selected by the Secretary and the Commandant to ensure that a realistic budget outlook does not censor necessary data on mission needs and tradeoffs. The report by the independent third party shall be provided to the Committee in conjunction with the President's fiscal year 2015 budget request. (Pages 85-86)

The section of H.R. 2217 as reported that appropriates funds for the Coast Guard's Acquisition, Construction, and Improvements (AC&I) account includes several provisos, including the following:

... *Provided,* That the funds provided by this Act shall be immediately available and allotted to contract for the production of the seventh National Security Cutter notwithstanding the availability of funds for post-production costs: *Provided further,* That the funds provided by this Act shall be immediately available and allotted to contract for long lead time materials, components, and designs for the eighth National Security Cutter notwithstanding the availability of funds for production costs or post-production costs:...

Section 517 of the bill as reported states:

Sec. 517. Any funds appropriated to Coast Guard `Acquisition, Construction, and Improvements' for fiscal years 2002, 2003, 2004, 2005, and 2006 for the 110-123 foot patrol boat conversion that are recovered, collected, or otherwise received as the result of negotiation, mediation, or litigation, shall be available until expended for the Fast Response Cutter program.

Section 570 of the bill as reported rescinds certain prior-year Coast Guard Acquisition, Construction, and Improvement (AC&I) account funding. S.Rept. 113-77 includes a table on page 189 showing these rescissions; the table does break down the rescinded amounts by individual line items within the AC&I account.

Appendix A. Findings and Recommendations of DHS Cutter Study

This appendix reprints the findings and recommendations of the August 2011 DHS Cutter study. They are as follows:

Findings

These are our major findings:

- **Replacing some NSCs with OPCs has a small, positive impact on OpEff [operational effectiveness].** Differences are on the order of 5 percent from POR [the program of record] and scale with the difference in cutter availability.

- **Replacing all OPCs with mod-270 has a significant positive impact on OpEff.** It increases drug interdiction by roughly 20 percent over POR. The increase in performance is much less than the increase in cutters. Performance in missions other than counter-drug and in regions outside the southeast is comparable to or slightly below POR.

- **Replacing OPCs with LCSs reduces OpEff significantly.** Given that LCS acquisition cost will be at least as much as OPC, we cannot construct a cost-effective way to use LCS to increase UCSG mission performance.

- **Moving away from POR adds uncertainty.** Reducing the number of NSCs may limit USCG ability to support defense operations (DEFOPS), and switching to a mod-270 [cutter design] creates a fleet that has trouble operating in poor weather.

- **Long-term total ownership cost is similar for all excursions.** Group B [alternative fleets 4, 5, and 6] is most expensive, due to higher personnel costs.

- **Updated or changed assumptions could change OpEff significantly.** More efficient patrol patterns could increase POR OpEff by 5 percentage points at no cost, while a potential "mid-capability" OPC could narrow the OpEff gap between group B and POR by another 5 percentage points. With both changes, group A [alternative fleets 1, 2, and 3] and group B should have about equal OpEff.

Recommendations

Based on our findings, we make the following recommendations.

- **USCG should quantify the DEFOPS requirement to assess the impact of reducing NSC numbers.** A 2.0 NSC presence will be difficult to support with only 5 NSC if they are also supporting other missions.

- **DHS PA&E should work with USCG to quantify distant, poor-weather operating areas to inform or mitigate the limitations of the mod-270.** Additional NSCs could offset some of the range and seakeeping deficiencies of the mod-270. Further study is necessary to see if it would be cost-effective.

- **DHS PA&E should explore additional fleet mix options.** Cost data should be updated as new information becomes available to confirm that the modeled excursions are still feasible. New options, such as a "mid-capability" OPC could improve fleet OpEff or decrease cost.

- **USCG should optimize its cutter basing and CONOPS.** Choosing cutter homeports and operating patterns to maximize on-station patrol time will get the most out of a cost-limited fleet.

- **DHS PA&E should commission a similar study for aircraft.** This study did not consider changes in aviation, which could have significant impact on performance. There may be opportunities to trade off air and surface assets to maximize total OpEff.

- **DHS PA&E should track long-term acquisition profiles and recapitalization priorities.** The multi-year spending profile for cutter acquisition has periods of significantly higher- and lower-than-average expenditure, which could have significant interplay with other DHS acquisition priorities.[86]

---

[86] Alarik Fritz, Raymond Gelhaus, and Kent Nordstrom, *Options for the Future USCG Cutter Fleet, Performance Trade-Offs with Fixed Acquisition Cost*, IPR 14297, August 2011, pp. 2-3.

Appendix B. P-5, P-40, and P-27 Data Exhibits for Littoral Combat Ship (LCS) Program

This appendix presents the Budget Item Justification Sheet (Exhibit P-40), Weapon System Cost Analysis sheet (Exhibit P-5), and Ship Production Schedule (Exhibit P-27) for the Navy's Littoral Combat Ship (LCS) program, as examples of the kind of information that is available each year to support congressional review and oversight of Navy shipbuilding programs.

Figure B-1. Budget Item Justification Sheet (Exhibit P-40)

For Navy Littoral Combat Ship (LCS) Program

CLASSIFICATION: UNCLASSIFIED

BUDGET ITEM JUSTIFICATION SHEET (P-40)
FY 2013 President's Budget

DATE: February 2012

APPROPRIATION/BUDGET ACTIVITY
SHIPBUILDING AND CONVERSION, NAVY/BA 2 Other Warships

P-1 LINE ITEM NOMENCLATURE
LITTORAL COMBAT SHIP (LCS)
BLI: 2127 / SUBHEAD NO.

(Dollars in Millions)	PRIOR YR	FY 2011	FY 2012	FY 2013	FY 2014	FY 2015	FY 2016	FY 2017	TO COMP	TOTAL PROG
QUANTITY	4	2	4	4	4	4	2	2	27	53
End Cost	2,434.3	1,162.6	1,634.0	1,785.0	1,819.6	1,881.5	1,013.0	896.0	17,582.4	30,386.4
Less Advance Procurement	0.0	0.0	78.9	0.0	0.0	0.0	0.0	0.0	0.0	78.9
Full Funding TOA	2,434.3	1,162.6	1,755.1	1,785.0	1,819.6	1,881.5	1,013.0	896.0	17,582.4	30,309.5
Plus Advance Procurement	0.0	78.9	0.0	0.0	0.0	0.0	0.0	0.0	0.0	78.9
Total Obligational Authority	2,434.3	1,241.5	1,755.1	1,785.0	1,819.6	1,881.5	1,013.0	896.0	17,582.4	30,388.4
Plus Outfitting / Plus Post Delivery	2.8	4.7	49.0	60.1	76.4	132.7	133.8	210.0	663.6	1,333.1
Total	2,437.1	1,246.2	1,804.1	1,845.1	1,896.0	2,014.2	1,146.8	1,106.0	18,226.0	31,721.5
Unit Cost (Ave. End Cost)	608.6	581.3	458.5	446.3	454.9	470.4	506.5	448.0	650.5	573.4

MISSION:

Provides for the design, construction, integration and testing of the Littoral Combat Ship (LCS) including Ordnance, Government Furnished Equipment (GFE), and includes Program Office and change order costs. LCS is a fast, agile, and networked surface combatant with capabilities optimized to defeat asymmetric threats, and assure naval and joint force access into contested littoral regions. It uses open-systems-architecture design, modular weapons, and sensor systems, and a variety of manned and unmanned vehicles to expand the battle space and project offensive power into the littoral. LCS operates with focused-mission packages that deploy manned and unmanned vehicles to execute a variety of missions, including littoral anti-submarine warfare (ASW), surface warfare (SUW), and mine countermeasures (MCM). LCS also possesses inherent capabilities, regardless of mission package installed, including Intelligence Surveillance Reconnaissance (ISR), homeland defense, Maritime Interdiction/Interception Operations (MIO), anti-terrorism/force protection (ATFP), air self-defense, joint littoral mobility, and logistic support for movement of personnel and supplies. This relatively small, high-speed surface combatant will complement the U.S. Navy's AEGIS fleet, by operating in environments where it is less desirable to employ larger, multi-mission ships. It can deploy independently to overseas littoral regions, remain on station for extended periods of time either with a battle group or through a forward-basing arrangement and is capable of underway replenishment. It will operate with Carrier Strike Groups, Surface Action Groups, in groups of other similar ships, or independently for diplomatic and presence missions. Additionally, it can operate cooperatively with the U.S. Coast Guard and Allies.

Characteristics	LM		GD/AUSTAL		
Overall Length:	115.3m		127.6m		
Max Beam:	17.5m		31.6m		
Displacement	3089 mt		2842 mt		
Production Status:	FY11	FY11	FY12	FY12	FY12
	LCS 7	LCS 8	LCS 9	LCS 10	LCS 11
Contract Award Date	3/11	3/11	3/12	3/12	3/12
Months to Completion					
a) Contract Award to Delivery	49 months	43 months	47 months	41 months	53 months
b) Construction Start to Delivery	35 months	36 months	36 months	36 months	37 months
Delivery Date	4/15	10/14	2/16	8/15	8/16
Completion of Fitting Out	8/15	2/15	8/16	12/15	12/16
Obligation Work Limiting Date	7/16	1/16	5/17	11/16	11/17

	FY12	FY13	FY13	FY13	FY13	FY13
Production Status:	LCS 12	LCS 13	LCS 14	LCS 15	LCS 16	
Contract Award Date	3/12	3/13	3/13	3/13	3/13	
a) Contract Award to Delivery	48 months	47 months	41 months	53 months	48 months	
b) Construction Start to Delivery	36 months	36 months	35 months	38 months	35 months	
Delivery Date	3/16	2/17	8/16	8/17	1/17	
Completion of Fitting Out	7/16	8/17	12/16	12/17	5/17	
Obligation Work Limiting Date	8/17	5/18	11/17	11/18	4/18	

Source: *Department of the Navy Fiscal Year (FY) 2013 Justification of Estimates, Shipbuilding and Conversion, Navy, February 2012, p. 11-1 (pdf page 156 of 246).*

Figure B-2. Weapon System Cost Analysis Sheet (Exhibit P-5)

For Navy Littoral Combat Ship (LCS) Program

CLASSIFICATION: UNCLASSIFIED
APPROPRIATION: SHIPBUILDING AND CONVERSION, NAVY

P-5 EXHIBIT
FY 2013 President's Budget
February 2012

WEAPON SYSTEM COST ANALYSIS (EXHIBIT P-5)
(Dollars in Thousands)

BUDGET ACTIVITY: 2
Other Warships

SUBHEAD NO. BLI: 2127

P-1 LINE ITEM NOMENCLATURE
LITTORAL COMBAT SHIP (LCS)

ELEMENT OF COST	FY 2009		FY 2010		FY 2011		FY 2012		FY 2013	
	QTY	COST	QTY	COST	QTY	COST	QTY	COST	QTY	COST
PLAN COSTS	2	36,603	2	24,438	2	91,386	4	83,459	4	83,989
BASIC CONST/CONVERSION		1,138,316		955,325		809,749		1,485,671		1,453,694
CHANGE ORDERS		38,610		45,950		43,100		82,100		72,684
ELECTRONICS		21,677		26,992		27,245		55,417		56,350
HM&E		4,595		5,908		6,806		13,843		14,078
OTHER COST		106,761		1,000		166,942		76,927		67,038
ORDNANCE		11,090		17,056		17,300		36,625		37,126
TOTAL SHIP ESTIMATE		1,357,652		1,076,669		1,162,528		1,834,042		1,784,959
LESS ADVANCE PROCUREMENT FY12		340,700						78,949		
LESS SCN AND MATERIALS TRANSFER FY06										
NET P-1 LINE ITEM:		1,016,952		1,076,669		1,162,528		1,755,093		1,784,959

Source: *Department of the Navy Fiscal Year (FY) 2013 Justification of Estimates, Shipbuilding and Conversion, Navy,* February 2012, p. 11-2 (pdf page 157 of 246).

Figure B-3. Ship Production Schedule (Exhibit P-27)

For Navy Littoral Combat Ship (LCS) Program

CLASSIFICATION: UNCLASSIFIED

SHIPBUILDING AND CONVERSION, NAVY
SHIP PRODUCTION SCHEDULE

EXHIBIT P-27
FY 2013 President's Budget
DATE:
February 2012

SHIP TYPE	HULL NUMBER	SHIPBUILDER	FISCAL YEAR AUTHORIZED	CONTRACT AWARD	START OF CONSTRUCTION	DELIVERY DATE
LCS	3	LOCKHEED MARTIN	09	MAR-09	APR-09	JUN-12
LCS	4	GD/AUSTAL	09	MAY-09	OCT-09	MAR-13
LCS	5	LOCKHEED MARTIN	10	DEC-10	JUL-11	AUG-14
LCS	6	AUSTAL	10	DEC-10	JUN-11	JUN-14
LCS	7	LOCKHEED MARTIN	11	MAR-11	MAY-12	APR-15
LCS	8	AUSTAL	11	MAR-11	OCT-11	OCT-14
LCS	9	LOCKHEED MARTIN	12	MAR-12	MAR-13	FEB-16
LCS	10	AUSTAL	12	MAR-12	SEP-12	AUG-15
LCS	11	LOCKHEED MARTIN	12	MAR-12	AUG-13	AUG-16
LCS	12	AUSTAL	12	MAR-12	APR-13	MAR-16
LCS	13	LOCKHEED MARTIN	13	MAR-13	MAR-14	FEB-17
LCS	14	AUSTAL	13	MAR-13	SEP-13	AUG-16
LCS	15	LOCKHEED MARTIN	13	MAR-13	AUG-14	AUG-17
LCS	16	AUSTAL	13	MAR-13	FEB-14	JAN-17
LCS	17	LOCKHEED MARTIN	14	MAR-14	MAR-15	FEB-18
LCS	18	AUSTAL	14	MAR-14	OCT-14	JUL-17
LCS	19	LOCKHEED MARTIN	14	MAR-14	AUG-15	AUG-18
LCS	20	AUSTAL	14	MAR-14	FEB-15	DEC-17
LCS	21	LOCKHEED MARTIN	15	MAR-15	MAR-16	FEB-19
LCS	22	AUSTAL	15	MAR-15	SEP-15	JUL-18
LCS	23	LOCKHEED MARTIN	15	MAR-15	AUG-16	AUG-19
LCS	24	AUSTAL	15	MAR-15	FEB-16	NOV-18
LCS	25	TBD	16	MAR-16	MAR-17	FEB-20
LCS	26	TBD	16	MAR-16	SEP-16	JUL-19
LCS	27	TBD	17	MAR-17	SEP-17	JUL-20
LCS	28	TBD	17	MAR-17	MAR-18	FEB-21

Source: *Department of the Navy Fiscal Year (FY) 2013 Justification of Estimates, Shipbuilding and Conversion, Navy,* February 2012, p. 11-2 (pdf page 159 of 246).

Appendix C. Navy Ship Force Structure Objective

Table C-1 presents the Navy's current ship force structure objective.

Table C-1. Navy Ship Force Structure Goal

Ship type	Force Structure Objective
Ballistic missile submarines (SSBNs)	12
Cruise missile submarines (SSGNs)	0
Attack submarines (SSNs)	48
Aircraft carriers	11
Cruisers and destroyers	88
Littoral Combat Ships (LCSs)	52
Amphibious ships	33
Combat logistics (resupply) ships	29
Joint High Speed Vessels (JHSVs)	10
Other (includes support ships)	23
Total battle force ships	**306**

Sources: Department of the Navy, *Report to Congress [on] Navy Combatant Vessel Force Structure Requirement,* January 2013, 3 pp. The cover letters for the report were dated January 31, 2013.

Appendix D. Navy FY2014 Five-Year Shipbuilding Plan

Table D-1 presents the Navy's FY2014 five-year (FY2014-FY2018) shipbuilding plan.

Table D-1. Navy FY2014 Five-Year (FY2014-FY2018) Shipbuilding Plan
(Battle force ships—i.e., ships that count against 306-ship goal)

Ship type	FY14	FY15	FY16	FY17	FY18	Total
Ford (CVN-78) class aircraft carrier					1	1
Virginia (SSN-774) class attack submarine	2	2	2	2	2	10
Arleigh Burke (DDG-51) class destroyer	1	2	2	2	2	9
Littoral Combat Ship (LCS)	4	4	2	2	2	14
LHA(R) amphibious assault ship	0	0	0	1	0	1
Fleet tug (TATF)	0	0	0	2	1	3
Mobile Landing Platform (MLP)/Afloat Forward Staging Base (AFSB)	1	0	0	0	0	1
TAO(X) oiler	0	0	1	0	1	2
TOTAL	**8**	**8**	**7**	**9**	**9**	**41**

Source: FY2014 Navy budget submission.

Notes: The MLP/AFSB is a variant of the MLP with additional features permitting it to serve in the role of an AFSB.

Appendix E. Navy FY2014 30-Year Shipbuilding Plan

Table E-1 shows the Navy's proposed FY2014 30-year (FY2014-FY2043) shipbuilding plan.

Table E-1. Navy FY2014 30-Year (FY2014-FY2043) Shipbuilding Plan

FY	CVN	LSC	SSC	SSN	SSBN	AWS	CLF	Supt	Total
14		1	4	2				1	8
15		2	4	2					8
16		2	2	2			1		7
17		2	2	2		1		2	9
18	1	2	2	2			1	1	9
19		2	3	2		1	1	1	10
20		2	3	2			1	2	10
21		2	3	2	1	1	1		10
22		3	3	2			1	2	11
23	1	3	3	2		1	1	3	14
24		2	3	1	1	1	1	2	11
25		3	3	2		1	1	1	11
26		2	1	1	1		1		6
27		3		2	1	1	1		8
28	1	3		1	1	2	1	1	10
29		3		1	1	1	1	1	8
30		2	1	1	1	1	1	2	9
31		2		2	1	1	1	2	9
32		2	1	1	1	2	1	3	11
33	1	2		1	1	1	1	2	9
34		2	1	1	1			2	7
35		2	1	1	1				5
36		2		1		1			4
37		2	4	2					8
38	1	3	4	2					10
39		3	4	1					8
40		3	4	2		2			11
41		3	4	1					8
42		3	3	2		1			9
43	1	2	3	1			1		8

Source: FY2014 30-year (FY2014-FY2043) shipbuilding plan.

Key: FY = Fiscal Year; **CVN** = aircraft carriers; **LSC** = surface combatants (i.e., cruisers and destroyers); **SSC** = small surface combatants (i.e., Littoral Combat Ships [LCSs]); **SSN** = attack submarines; **SSGN** = cruise missile submarines; **SSBN** = ballistic missile submarines; **AWS** = amphibious warfare ships; **CLF** = combat logistics force (i.e., resupply) ships; **Supt** = support ships.

Table E-2 shows the Navy's projection of force levels for FY2014-FY2043 that would result from implementing the FY2014 30-year (FY2014-FY2043) shipbuilding plan shown in **Table E-1**.

Table E-2. Projected Force Levels Resulting from FY2014 30-Year (FY2014-FY2043) Shipbuilding Plan

	CVN	LSC	SSC	SSN	SSGN	SSBN	AWS	CLF	Supt	Total
306 ship plan	11	88	52	48	0	12	33	29	33	306
FY14	10	85	26	55	4	14	31	31	26	282
FY15	10	78	23	55	4	14	28	29	29	270
FY16	11	82	27	53	4	14	29	29	31	280
FY17	11	83	29	50	4	14	30	29	33	283
FY18	11	84	33	52	4	14	31	29	33	291
FY19	11	86	38	52	4	14	31	29	35	300
FY20	11	87	37	49	4	14	31	29	33	295
FY21	11	88	37	49	4	14	31	29	33	296
FY22	12	87	39	48	4	14	31	29	33	297
FY23	12	87	38	48	4	14	31	29	34	297
FY24	12	89	40	48	4	14	32	29	34	302
FY25	11	88	42	47	4	14	34	29	34	303
FY26	11	89	45	46	2	14	33	29	33	302
FY27	11	91	48	45	1	13	33	29	33	304
FY28	11	90	51	43	0	12	33	29	33	302
FY29	11	88	52	42	0	11	33	29	33	299
FY30	11	86	52	43	0	11	32	29	33	297
FY31	11	82	52	44	0	11	32	29	33	294
FY32	11	81	52	45	0	10	32	29	34	294
FY33	11	81	52	46	0	10	33	29	34	296
FY34	11	80	52	47	0	10	34	29	34	297
FY35	11	82	52	48	0	10	33	29	34	299
FY36	11	84	52	50	0	10	33	29	34	303
FY37	11	86	52	51	0	10	34	29	33	306
FY38	11	88	52	50	0	10	33	29	34	307
FY39	11	90	52	50	0	10	33	29	33	308
FY40	10	90	52	50	0	10	32	29	33	308
FY41	10	90	52	49	0	11	33	29	33	307
FY42	10	88	52	51	0	12	32	29	33	307
FY43	10	88	52	51	0	12	31	29	33	306

Source: FY2014 30-year (FY2014-FY2043) shipbuilding plan.

Note: Figures for support ships include five JHSVs transferred from the Army to the Navy and operated by the Navy primarily for the performance of Army missions.

Key: FY = Fiscal Year; **CVN** = aircraft carriers; **LSC** = surface combatants (i.e., cruisers and destroyers); **SSC** = small surface combatants (i.e., frigates, Littoral Combat Ships [LCSs], and mine warfare ships); **SSN** = attack submarines; **SSGN** = cruise missile submarines; **SSBN** = ballistic missile submarines; **AWS** = amphibious warfare ships; **CLF** = combat logistics force (i.e., resupply) ships; **Supt** = support ships.

Author Contact Information

Ronald O'Rourke
Specialist in Naval Affairs
rorourke@crs.loc.gov, 7-7610

www.ingramcontent.com/pod-product-compliance
Lightning Source LLC
Chambersburg PA
CBHW080539290526
45790CB00006B/2471

* 9 7 8 1 5 0 3 2 7 8 3 9 4 *